Diverse Perspectives
School Communities

What is an inclusive school community?

How do stakeholders perceive their roles and responsibilities towards inclusive school communities?

How can school communities become more inclusive through engagement with individual perspectives?

Diverse Perspectives on Inclusive School Communities captures and presents the voices of a wide range of stakeholders including young people and their parents, teachers, support staff, educational psychologists, social workers, health practitioners and volunteers in producing a collection of varied perspectives on inclusive education.

In this fascinating book, Tsokova and Tarr uniquely assemble a compilation of accounts collected through in-depth interviews with over twenty-five participants, met throughout the course of their professional lives. The authors focus on how we can ensure *all* children receive the best education and social provision in inclusive school communities.

Key learning points in this book emphasise:

- links between early life and educational experiences;
- constructions of inclusion;
- an understanding of roles and responsibilities;
- the power of agency in relation to inclusive school communities.

The text contributes to current debates surrounding educational policy initiatives, highlighting similarities and differences across people and professions, and illuminating a way forward for the consideration of a broader range of insight into the concept of inclusion and ways this can be achieved. Including both UK and international perspectives that illustrate different stages of the inclusive education process, this text will be invaluable to anyone affiliated with inclusive schooling in a personal or professional capacity.

Diana Tsokova is Lecturer in Psychology and Special Needs in Primary Education at the Institute of Education, University of London.

Jane Tarr is Associate Head of Department for Childhood and Education Studies at the University of the West of England, Bristol.

Diverse Perspectives on Inclusive School Communities

Diana Tsokova and Jane Tarr

Routledge
Taylor & Francis Group

LONDON AND NEW YORK

First published 2012
by Routledge
2 Park Square, Milton Park, Abingdon, Oxon OX14 4RN

Simultaneously published in the USA and Canada
by Routledge
711 Third Avenue, New York, NY 10017

Routledge is an imprint of the Taylor & Francis Group, an informa business

British Library Cataloguing in Publication Data
A catalogue record for this book is available from the British Library

Library of Congress Cataloging in Publication Data
  Diverse perspectives on inclusive school communities/Diana
  Tsokova, Jane Tarr.
    p. cm.
  ISBN 978-0-415-59457-8 (hardback) — ISBN 978-0-415-59458-5 —
  ISBN 978-0-203-11259-5   1. Inclusive education.   2. Educational
  equalization.   3. Children with disabilities—Education.   I. Tarr,
  Jane.   II. Title.
  LC1200.T76 2012
  371.9'046—dc23
                                                    2011052176

ISBN: 978-0-415-59457-8 (hbk)
ISBN: 978-0-415-59458-5 (pbk)
ISBN: 978-0-203-11259-5 (ebk)

Typeset in Bembo
by RefineCatch Ltd, Bungay, Suffolk

MIX
Paper from
responsible sources
FSC   FSC® C004839
www.fsc.org

Printed and bound in Great Britain by
TJ International Ltd, Padstow, Cornwall

I dedicate this book to all the children labelled autistic with whom I have worked during my career – with gratitude for teaching me so much and for the love they brought into my life.

Diana Tsokova

I dedicate this book to my dear brother Alex, who passed away on the day that our book proposal was approved.

Jane Tarr

Contents

List of figures   ix

Acknowledgements   xi

1 Introduction   **1**

The organisation of this book 2
Why research inclusive education and inclusive school communities
*   through perspectives? 3*
Theoretical framework 5
Methodology 6
Research process 7
Research ethics 8
Context 9

2 Stories   **21**

The stories of mothers and young people 21
Teachers' stories 35
Stories from support staff 48
Stories from governors/community members 55
Stories from educational psychologists 66
Stories from social workers 73
Stories from health practitioners 81
The authors' stories and reflections 92

3 Discussion of key learning points   **107**

Individual contributions 107
Concerns and complexities 110

Collective contribution 111
Inclusive school communities 115

References   117
Index   125

Figures

2.1 Cher's symbol of inclusion 29
3.1 Construct map derived from individual contributions 109
3.2 Theoretical framework and main themes 111
3.3 Concerns and complexities related to inclusion 112
3.4 School community hierarchy 114

Acknowledgements

We would like to thank a number of people who made this book possible. First and foremost, all the people who shared their stories with us and without whom this text would have been impossible: thank you for your trust, for your patience through the story verification process and for your unselfish commitment.

We would also like to thank Routledge for seeing the potential in our proposal and for their continuous support when we were faced with various personal obstacles.

We would like to thank Len Barton, Roger Slee and Gary Thomas, who have been inspirational in the development of our ideas. We would also like to thank Andrew Azzopardi who kindly shared some of his work and offered his 'virtual' friendly encouragement. It is impossible to mention everyone from the Institute of Education and the University of the West of England who in different ways have encouraged the emergence of this text. Our thanks go to Keith Pickton for his wonderful design work.

Last but not least, we would like to thank our loved ones for putting up with us throughout ups and downs, and our families for being there.

Chapter 1

Introduction

This text rests on two core concepts: inclusive education and inclusive school communities. Both the notions of inclusive education and inclusive school communities have been debated and contested in the academic and professional literature, amassing diverse perspectives and discourses. A broad focus on 'inclusion in education is concerned with increasing participation in and reducing exclusion from the learning opportunities cultures and communities of the mainstream . . . a deep view of participation and the development of a transformational rather than an assimilationist view of inclusion . . . We continue to identify inclusion with the development of comprehensive, community education (Booth and Potts, 1983)' (Booth, 2003: 2–3).

This book seeks to capture the voices of a wide range of stakeholders including children, young people and their families, educational, health, social care and other professionals, and representatives of the voluntary sector in contributing towards the development of inclusive school communities. The aim is to consider all those agencies involved with supporting the education and well-being of children and young people.

Inclusive education at the school community level emphasises the comprehensiveness of schools; it is concerned with ensuring that all learners have opportunities to engage in the same educational processes. An inclusive school community is concerned with 'providing the chance to share in the common wealth of the school and its culture' (Thomas 1998).

The core assumption in this book is that inclusive education and inclusive school communities are good for individuals and for our society. We approached our research with this underlying assumption but without imposing our conceptualisations on the people who took part. Our intention was to explore inclusive education and inclusive school communities through diverse perspectives incorporating examples of lived experiences.

In the title of our book, *Diverse Perspectives on Inclusive School Communities* and its composition, there are a number of other underlying assumptions. First, by claiming that we look at perspectives on inclusive school communities we assume that these exist and that the concept can be defined. On the other hand, we recognise the complexity and multidimensionality of the notion and the difficulty posed by diverse understanding of its meaning.

Most recently, a welcome special issue of the *International Journal of Inclusive Education* in February 2011 has been devoted to the understanding of inclusive school communities. Within this special issue, contributions from the UK, USA, Australia and other European countries have tried to debate and contextualise inclusive schools and communities. Important issues and questions have been raised to the role of schools in educating a diversity of students to participate in learning, community life and the broader society. With regard to the roles and responsibilities of professionals towards society as a whole (Curcic *et al.* 2011: 117–18), what may be their discernible roles and functions within a community, and on that basis, of inclusive communities (Azzopardi 2011b: 189)? Also debated are the processes by which educational professionals engage in and create communities of critical learners whilst examining and reviewing their beliefs and practices to embrace the needs of diverse learners within an inclusive school culture.

Some of these insights prompted our discussion about how inclusive school communities come to be conceptualised within this current text. Our perspective of inclusive school communities builds on the idea about extended schools where those professionals and community members who have major stakes in healthy development, well-being and education of children and young people are pulled together to enable every young learner to thrive and flourish in an inclusive society.

Azzopardi notes that 'whereas there are a number of compound discourses that are associated with the idea of community, a particularly important premise is that communities are cohesive. On the other hand, others claim that community in its own right is a value' (Azzopardi 2011a: 1).

Our understanding of school communities includes all stakeholders within the local community of people that schools serve. We recognise the value of schools as communities in their own right but believe that one of the most distinctive features of inclusive school communities is that they promote the sharing of fundamental values and purpose: the education of young and old for individual and collective well-being and advancement. We believe that where school communities are inclusive or strive to be inclusive there are positive outcomes both for individuals and for the communities. These emerge from the ethos of respect for difference, equality, social justice and social cohesion. We understand inclusive school communities as cohesive communities and we see inclusive education as one of the main ways to increase such social cohesion.

The organisation of this book

The assembled perspectives of stakeholders are presented in separate chapters to stimulate thinking about potential contributions in relation to roles and responsibilities towards inclusive school communities. Our understanding is that membership of inclusive school communities is fluid, but within the limitations of this book we focus on a small number of stakeholders across a range of disciplines and areas of life.

We begin with an overview of the international, UK and professional discipline-related policy contexts in order to set the scene for the following chapters. Such contextualisation is intended to enhance understanding of individual experience within the stories. Our rationale for sequenced presentation of the stories rests in a central focus on immediate stakeholders in a school gradually drawing in representatives of related professional disciplines. We begin with the stories of mothers and children who are central to the educational enterprise and finish with our own.

We are drawing mainly on unrelated individuals belonging to stakeholders' collective agencies, recognising that such collectives are complex: backgrounds, roles and responsibilities inevitably overlap. Some of the individuals whose perspectives are included in this book are related, for example the participating disabled young people and their mothers. The presentation of their perspectives in Chapter 2 aims to enhance understanding of their specific contexts without undermining individuality and uniqueness of standpoint.

Why research inclusive education and inclusive school communities through perspectives?

Throughout our professional life we have been reflecting on our personal and professional experiences and recognised the impact that these have on our constantly evolving conceptual understanding. We came to understand the value of this process for our learning, and as teacher educators we encourage other learners to engage with and reflect on their own personal histories, and recognise significant experiences that had influences on their conceptual understanding. We argue for breadth of experiences – across the diversity of people, cultures, learning environments and capacities – together with critical reflection to enhance learning. In our teacher education practices we draw upon our own, pupils', parents', student teachers', students' and professionals' stories to support learning. In our experience, such an approach to learning has been particularly powerful as an example of inclusive pedagogy. This text and the process of writing is another expression of this inclusive approach to learning. In our view, we hope this reflective process has transformative potential and can both challenge assumptions and support re-conceptualisation.

In the process of exploration of stakeholders' perspectives, we created an ongoing dialogue between ourselves and the people who contributed to this book. In addition, we hope to create opportunities for the readers of this book to engage in this dialogue.

Lynn Raphael Reed (2010) in a seminar presentation about dialogic and respectful communities cited Sidorkin who, drawing on the work of

Buber (1959) and Bakhtin (1981), argues that this kind of dialogue is at the basis of human being and existence stating that we are

> truly human only when we are in dialogical relation with another. The most important things in human lives happen between human beings, rather than within or without them . . . for full existence as a human being, one not only has to enter the dialogical relation, but also to know and value the fact of such an entry.
>
> (Sidorkin 1999: 11–13)

This supports our understanding of inclusive education as communication and dialogue between different learners.

Slee proposes an agenda for collective action that includes restorative, analytic, policy, education and values related tasks with specific elements and actions. As a part of the values task he emphasises the need to establish 'communities that recognise, represent, authorise and learn from difference' (Slee 2011: 168). This is also set out as one of the main principles in Touraine, underpinning the possibilities for a 'school for the Subject' where 'the education gives a central importance to diversity (both historical and cultural) and to recognition of the Other . . . and encourages every possible form of intercultural communication' (Touraine 2000: 270).

In this text we emphasise the individual perspective, personal and educational experiences, and reflection on these; confidence in speaking out and then listening to others. Integral here is the element of trust which develops through personal connection and shared experiences. This sharing and understanding of own and others' meanings with consideration of the personal and interpersonal contexts enable new insights and knowledge to develop. This is supported by Sidorkin (1999: 17–18) when talking about human beings relating to each other through a 'dialogue' in the deepest sense of this word. This means an affective as well as intellectual engagement that allows us to transcend beyond the situational into a 'meta' and multi-dimensional perspective that reflects the 'polyphonic' voice. He suggests that such an interaction goes 'beyond discourse' into 'polyphony':

> The distinctive voices of the polyphonic truth do not merge and do not come to a consensus . . . voices must achieve a state when they are truly and fully addressed to each other. This means that the voices argue each other's real, and not imagined positions.
>
> (ibid.: 30)

Such dialogue serves as a foundation for negotiation and a precondition for a democratic decision-making process about how to make school communities more inclusive and ultimately endorses the value of democratic comprehensive education.

Grossman (2008: 39) draws attention to the need for opportunities to practise democratic values through the involvement not solely of those already 'secured within the mainstream . . . but by those not secured and not privileged.' This author believes that 'this is a powerful argument for inclusive societies and inclusive schools to serve them' (ibid.).

In our approach to this book we aimed to engage with as many and as diverse perspectives as possible; therefore, we aimed to research inclusive education and inclusive school communities in an inclusive way.

Theoretical framework

Oliver suggests that socially produced knowledge based on the experience of oppressed groups has to play an increasingly important part in 'all knowledge production' through 'research based upon the discourse of production.' Further, he emphasises that 'this may eventually lead to the fusion of knowledge and research production into a single coherent activity in which we produce ourselves and our worlds in ways which will make us all truly human' (Oliver 2002: 15).

Thinking about disability, difference and diversity in the last thirty years has undergone a significant paradigmatic shift. In recent years this has been demonstrated by a movement away from 'within the child' interpretations of difficulty and disability to increasing consideration of the existing barriers in the social environment from micro to meso, exo and macro systems in Bronfenbrenner's (1979) terms. In relation to inclusive education, the emerging new paradigms suggest different solutions: in educational practice this is demonstrated through a move away from special education to looking at transformation of schools as institutions, and at the society as a whole in order to accommodate all learners.

This study adopts a social constructivist approach, viewing disability, inclusion and inclusive school communities as socially constructed phenomena. We draw on the social model of disability (Oliver 1990, 1994, 1996; Oliver and Barnes 1998) seeking to explore and understand difference and diversity in context, and on disability emancipatory research (Barnes 2002; Oliver 2002), with an emphasis on the rights of oppressed groups of people to have a voice and to uncover the barriers they are facing. Thus, Oliver (2002: 2–3) emphasises the political nature of the emancipatory paradigm in addition to seeing disability as a social problem.

The role of disability studies and emancipatory research has been promoted and maintained further by Barton through his own work and the journal *Disability & Society*.

Azzopardi argues that '"inclusion" needs to be viewed as a process located within the culture, policies and practices of a whole school and community' (Azzopardi 2008: 11). He therefore suggests that research into it should draw on an 'assortment of contexts: school, family, disabled and parent activists, policy-makers, service providers and trade unionists.' We are drawing on a similar breadth of perspectives.

Slee, too, endorses the importance of aiming for such an emancipatory worldview based in the analysis of the complex social factors in schools 'that more or less disable or enable children' (Slee 2011: 104).

By exploring the views of parents, children and professionals in education and beyond, we see a potential not only for knowledge production and development but also for transformation and change in policy and practice. We aim to apply these theoretical frameworks through recognition, valuing and enabling space for diverse perspectives, learning and a democratic dialogue.

Methodology

We draw upon individual perspectives on lived experiences and critical event narratives, arguing that such a methodological approach holds the potential to enrich insights into inclusive school communities. We hope that the resulting insight becomes a broad conversation about conceptualisation of inclusive education and its manifestations in individuals' lived experiences. In creating such a dialogic space for ourselves and those we engaged with, it was intended that we reflected the very principles we are researching in relation to inclusive school communities. The process was intended to become mutu-ally enriching and reflective learning for all.

We committed to gather people's perspectives on inclusion and inclusive school communities through a methodology that recognises differences, enables each person to contribute and respects divergence of viewpoints. It is understood that some groups of people have less powerful voices and this research seeks to draw a range of voices together in an equitable manner.

Young maintains that 'narrative' as a research method carries such potential, because

> narrative empowers relatively disenfranchised groups to assert themselves publicly; it also offers means by which people whose experi-ences and beliefs differ so much that they do not share enough premises to engage in fruitful debate can never the less, reach dialogic under-standing.
>
> (Young 2000: 53)

> It was intended that the stories we crafted will provide children, mothers, professionals and paraprofessionals with 'an opportunity of telling someone how they see the world.'
>
> (Stenhouse 1978: 222)

Research process

In the research process we engaged in a dialogue with over thirty people. Three or four stories for each stakeholder section were included in the final text with the exception of those of the mothers and young people, which we have combined. We met all of these people in our professional lives in the last fifteen years. They come from a range of different cultural backgrounds, ages, gender, sexual orientation and marital status.

Each person was approached and asked to share their perspective based on individual experience with education and inclusion. We asked for examples of critical events that people perceived as influential in shaping their understanding of inclusion. We anticipated that within the breadth of the subject matter and the limits of the book contract it may be impossible and impractical to attempt to collect coherent life stories. Therefore we prepared some core questions/topics around which conversations took place. The questions we asked aimed to prompt conversations around the following:

* understanding of inclusive education;
* critical examples of inclusion;
* perceived roles and responsibilities in relation to inclusive school communities;
* understanding of current policy developments and their impact on experience.

Each conversation was recorded by the interviewer, transcribed and shared again with the person we talked to for confirmation. In some cases a more discursive process took place at the end of the story to highlight specific examples and thoughts.

It is intended that through a reflection upon life experiences, each person might recognise and perhaps gain a deeper insight into the importance of their agency within the political nature of inclusive school communities. In this way an empowering and new socially mediated perspective may emerge that enables all involved to recognise their political power, described by Casey as 'a reconceptualisation of what is meant by political. Central to the definition is the recognition that the personal is political and, further, that power is exercised in all relationships, not just those connected to the state' (Casey 1995: 223).

Our knowledge of the people who took part in this research has been beneficial in gaining a deeper insight into their perceptions and world views. For those we knew less well this insight came as a result of the conversation, and usually towards the end of the meeting. We used the transcripts of the collected perspectives to craft a story for each person. The crafted stories include some common components:

- early life experiences
- professional experiences
- understanding of role and responsibilities
- concept of inclusion
- contribution to inclusive school communities.

We did not apply these rigidly but worked from the transcripts. Some of the stories incorporate all these aspects, and others just some. In addition, they do not appear in the same order, as we aimed to achieve a coherent and honest account. All crafted stories were offered for verification by the people who shared them, although not every person took up on this. Nevertheless, at least three-quarters of the stories were verified.

Research ethics

Such an approach to gaining understanding about inclusive school communities can be ethically challenging; Griffiths (2003) has sought to clarify whether research is 'on/for/with people.' We faced this challenge by positioning ourselves as storytellers and learners in the whole research process. For this purpose we have included our own stories and reflections at the end of this text. In addition, by the virtue of our professional status as lecturers in higher education we recognise our status as stakeholders in the promotion of inclusive school communities. We recognise that as academics we are privileged in that we have been given the opportunity to write and publish this book, and therefore to make important decisions not only about what and how to research but also who to include.

What is more, Stanley and Wise (1993) write about ethical dilemmas of this kind as the researchers construct the interview framework and thereby the nature of how participants are encouraged to share their stories. In our case, where possible, negotiation took place with each person at various stages of the research process. We approached people with an outline of our aims and motivation for this book and invited them to take part in the research. We gained written consent from each person, including the young people. Conversations with young people took place in their homes in the presence of their mothers. The consent forms include assurances of anonymity and confidentiality. Most of the names used in this book are fictional and there are some real first names only. Names of places, organisations and people within each story are initialled. At the point of consent, people were told of their continuing opportunities to engage in the verification process. We exercised our own professional judgement and excluded parts of some conversations from the stories where we considered that these carry potential risks to individuals implicated.

Where discrepancies emerged, these have been resolved and we believe the final chapters include the agreed perspective of each of those whose story was included.

In seeking a diverse group of people, we were not matching experiences with our own. We attempted to display respect and empathy with all those we talked to, regardless of their backgrounds and characteristics, to ensure that they felt fully comfortable and included in the process of research.

Context

The current context of political and ideological change impacts upon the way we approach the educational provision for all learners. Therefore, the process of inclusion within school communities cannot be fully understood without a consideration of the wider social and political context.

The changing global community is influenced by competing forces that bring people together and create tensions between them. Within global processes a variety of factors impact upon aspects of social cohesion such as migration, pluralism, financial crises, environmental disasters and continued levels of poverty (Green *et al.* 2006). Inclusion is continuously present and endorsed in the global educational agenda as evidenced in the United Nations Convention on Children's Rights (UNCRC) (United Nations 1989), the Salamanca Statement (United Nations Educational, Scientific and Cultural Organization (UNESCO) 1994) and the United Nations Convention on the Rights of Persons with Disability (United Nations 2006). These international documents at least firmly define the place of inclusion as a global task.

In the European context, there are specific working groups focused on social cohesion and understanding of intercultural communication and dialogue. The programme of social cohesion set up in 1998 by the Council of Europe Committee of Ministers sought to implement a strategy for social cohesion aimed at analysis of changes taking place in society and their consequences for social exclusion/inclusion. The aim was to influence attitudes and assist policy development for member states that took social cohesion and inclusion into social and educational practice.

On a national level, in the UK educational legislation had previously focused predominantly on children with special educational needs (SEN) and dis-abilities when looking to promote inclusive education. More recently, consideration of differences in ethnicity and religion has resulted in policy developments to achieve community cohesion. The UK response to the aspirations to the UNCRC eventually led to the Every Child Matters (Department for Education and Skills (DfES) 2004) agenda, which adopted a more holistic approach to provision for children, young people and their families. Such developments sit alongside the final report of the Commission on Integration and Cohesion, 'Our Shared Future' (Communities and Local Government (CLG) 2006), which explored the processes of community social cohesion. Eventually this emerged as a duty placed on schools to promote community cohesion (Department for Children, Schools and Families (DCSF)/CLG 2007), emphasised by the Diversity and Citizenship Curriculum Review

(DfES 2007a), asking them to address the questions of how we live together and how we deal with difference.

In the 1970s, social policy sought to ensure protection for the rights of those of different sex, race and faith, followed in the 1990s by legislation for those with disability, and in the 2000s by legislation to protect different ages and sexuality. The 2010 Equality Act has recognised this fragmentation and drawn this range of characteristics together under one legislative framework that has enabled nine characteristics to be recognised and protected from discrimination (The Stationery Office (TSO) 2010).

Inclusive school communities today have a much broader set of responsibilities to engender understanding between a wide range of different groups.

Inclusive education

1970 saw the first legal requirement in the UK for all children to be educated in schools, which led on to the Warnock Report (1978) and subsequent Education Act (1981) that introduced the concept of SEN and recognised that, from an educational point of view, learners may have SEN of varying degrees. On the basis of Lady Warnock's recommendations, three aspects of integration were defined – locational, social and functional (1978).

The early 1990s saw increasing focus on rights for parents and the setting up of frameworks for parent and school partnerships. In 1994 the UNESCO Salamanca statement was very influential in promoting conceptions of inclusive education, clearly stating that 'regular schools with this inclusive orientation are the most effective means of combating discriminatory attitudes, creating welcoming communities, building an inclusive society and achieving education for all' (UNESCO 1994). The education minister in the late 1990s, David Blunkett, was determined to encourage disabled children to learn alongside their peers as far as possible and developed policy throughout the next ten years to bring the Disability Discrimination Act (1995) into the educational context by 2005. The Special Educational Needs Code of Practice (DfES 2001) acknowledged the value of listening to the voice of the child, in working closely with parents and in operating in partnership with a range of different agencies to support the child and their family.

Legislation currently expects all schools to have schemes and action plans (the Special Educational Needs and Disability Act, 2001; the Disability Discrimination Act, 2005; the Equality Act, 2010) that outline how they are meeting the duty to include all learners, with reasonable adjustments in place, and how they are monitoring the impact of inclusive policies for disabled pupils and protected characteristics in general.

The recent coalition government in UK has produced a Green Paper (Department for Education (DfE) 2011b) opening up to consultation at present around provision for learners with SEN and proposing to introduce a single assessment process as an Education, Health and Care Plan by 2014, to include the option of a personal budget for such families, aspiring to give parents a 'real' choice of which school their child attends.

Listening to the learner

The UNCRC outlined the rights of all children and gradually led to changes in the way adults and children relate to each other. Every four years, governments are expected to report on the progress they have made in relation to the forty-two articles in the convention. The UK took some time to respond formally to these rights, resulting in the Every Child Matters: Change for children (DfES 2004) giving children and families considerably more attention.

Practitioners working with challenging learners have explored a wide range of approaches to hearing the voice of the child, resulting in a far more child-focused provision in some cases. 'The child's voice' has increasingly become a focus of attention in academic research and publications (Alderson 2008; Flutter and Ruddock 2004). The aim is to bring about change in the education systems as a result of such voice.

In an attempt to learn about the student voice in one school context, Gunter and Thomas found that pupils' role is often to respond to the work-ings of the system. Instead, their research suggests

> that students like to learn and associate with others, and that they can be policy makers and not just policy takers in school. They can take on tough issues to resolve the issues that matter to them, and they can research, make and implement policy.
>
> (Gunter and Thomas 2007)

The voices of children and young people with SEN are frequently more chal-lenging to hear. Several researchers have explored approaches to gaining access to their voices and found them to be highly illuminating (MacConville 2007; Armstrong 2003; Beresford *et al.* 2007).

The role of the parent

Since the Warnock Report (1978), the rights and perspectives of parents of children with SEN have been debated in relation to education policy and practice. The following plethora of educational legislation resulting in the current legislative framework has increasingly endorsed parents' involvement and contribution to the education of their children. The role of parents as partners in the education of children with SEN became even stronger through the Every Child Matters agenda and in the Children's Plan (DCSF 2007). The DfES under Labour Government produced the *Every Parent Matters* (DfES 2007b) booklet and guidance on parental involvement and home–school agreements. In addition, the Department published examples of good practice. Research over the last thirty years has drawn attention to the complexities around parent partnerships with education in practice (Wolfendale 1997, 2002; Allan 2008; Schneider 2007; Elkins *et al.* 2003; Pinkus 2003; Cole 2004, 2007; Frederickson and Cline 2009; Dukes 2007).

Where barriers to partnership with parents have been identified, these situate mostly along the attitudinal, informational, communicational, economic and social domains (Parents as Partners in Early Learning (PPEL) 2007). Parents are often seen to be caught in a system where, despite increased policy developments, their rights are not guaranteed and their roles become increasingly demanding in fighting for scarce resources in ensuring that their children's educational needs are being met – fights that not all families can keep up with. As Allan notes,

> Parents' confusion over inclusion arises from being denied information about provision for disabled youngsters and from being generally discouraged from challenging education authorities and schools when they have concerns about provision.
>
> (Allan 2008: 11)

More recently, the Lamb Inquiry (2009) reflected a number of stumbling blocks facing parents who struggle to ensure adequate provision for their children. Yet, as Mittler (2008) rightfully points out, winning parents for the cause of inclusive education could be perceived as one of the biggest challenges facing inclusive education in the twenty-first century.

The reality of widespread educational practices masquerading as inclusion but offering no real accommodation, let alone transformation, of mainstream education has left parents with no real choice but a long list of dilemmas. Parents' dissatisfaction with this reality has been used to inform what was termed and critiqued as a U-turn on the philosophy of inclusive education (see Warnock 2005). In his response to Warnock's 'new look,' Barton (2005) critiqued her for the displayed lack of regard to twenty-five years of research and scholarly publications in the field of inclusive education along with a lack of recognition for the struggles of disabled people.

Mothers, too, struggle to get their perspectives across and to effect necessary systemic changes despite the increased policy emphasis on their rights and responsibilities. Cole points out that the dominant discourse of 'parents as partners' whose voices are important does little to disturb the existing boundary between 'the public professionals and private parents.' She maintains that the lack of attention to gender 'negates the voice of personal experience and prioritizes the professional and expert voice' (Cole 2007: 165).

Mothers are in a unique position where their commitment to secure quality education of their child is part of what it means to be a parent. They have no choice but to engage in the education struggle regardless of their individual capacity to do so. More often than not these struggles are steered by existing legislation and provision towards the plane of identification of needs and school placement for their child, but this is where their power ends. They have very limited actual power to effect change at an institutional or classroom level. The control over classroom practice remains with teachers, and this comes through strongly in their shared experiences. Laluvein (2010: 195, 196), too, found that despite policy recommendations 'as to how parent–professional relations should be conducted', professional knowledge is often privileged over the knowledge that parents have, most of which is based in experience.

In the context of unprecedented cuts to the public sphere, the most recently published SEN Green Paper (DfE 2011b) of the coalition government takes this further by promising to redress the balance and give parents more choice and power through increasing and diversifying the 'segregated' end of the educational service continuum. It proposes to also give parents hold of the purse through individual pupil premiums. The big questions and tests to these proposals are yet to be posed and debated.

The role of the teacher

The current UK standards for qualified teachers at different stages of their professional development (Teacher Development Agency (TDA) 2008) all recognise the need for 'a commitment to collaborative and co-operative working' and for those excellent teachers an extensive 'knowledge on matters concerning equality, inclusion and diversity in teaching' is required (ibid.: Q6, E6). Newly qualified teachers are also expected to 'know how to take practical account of diversity and promote equality and inclusion in their teaching' (ibid.: Q19) and also to 'know and understand the roles of colleagues with specific responsibilities, including those with responsibility for learners with special educational needs and disabilities and other individual learning needs' (ibid.: Q20).

These standards for teachers are currently being revised, and for September 2012 expect all teachers regardless of their stages of professional development to have 'a clear understanding of the needs of all pupils, including those with special educational needs; those of high ability; those with English as an additional language; those with disabilities; and be able to use and evaluate distinctive teaching approaches to engage and support them.' The understanding of inter-professional working practices is included through the expectation for all teachers to 'develop effective professional relationships with colleagues, knowing how and when to draw on advice and specialist support; deploy support staff effectively' and also to 'communicate effectively with parents with regard to pupils' achievements and well-being' (TDA 2011).

Although the newly revised standards aim to unify the requirements for different levels of professional development, the earlier emphasis on equality, diversity and inclusion, together with collaborative working practices with other professionals, is notably missing. The earlier emphasis moved thinking from an individual professional engaged alone in a classroom, providing effective teaching and learning experiences for a group of pupils, to a more holistic process involving teachers working together with teaching assistants (TAs), learning support assistants (LSAs), professionals from health, social care, voluntary and community sectors and parents to enable a deeper understanding of the child. Such a team around the child holds the potential for insight into difference and diversity leading to a more inclusive school context. The forthcoming change of emphasis may impact negatively on the way schools develop as inclusive communities.

Despite the key role of teachers in inclusive education, and their broadening responsibilities as teachers for all, there is also a dearth of literature examining the changes in teachers' professional realities. The disability discrimination legislation's application to schools rests on the assumption that all teaching professionals understand and are able to enact the social model of disability and its implications for the changing philosophy of difference.

The paradigmatic shift required for truly inclusive education requires a re-conceptualisation not only of the role of the teacher but also about the role of education *per se* and the need to develop a more inclusive pedagogy. Teachers' understanding of their responsibility to all learners, their knowledge and skills capacity to educate all and work collaboratively with others, are key for an inclusive school community. Thomas and Loxley (2001) have rightfully pointed out that traditionally there exists a division between educational conceptions of inclusion and conceptions of social justice in terms of inclusion, which limits teachers' capacity to take on both aspects simultaneously.

Individual teachers require a context within which the social and the academic progress of all learners can be understood. This is the responsibility of everyone, yet perhaps more importantly of the school leadership team, having a most crucial role over structures and processes in the school community. How inclusive school communities are is largely dependent upon what structures and processes are put in place to support inclusivity.

Gunter and Thomas (2007: 185) emphasise the importance of the head teacher's role through the prevalence of a 'dominant discourse of a follower-based organizational culture through head teacher leadership, vision and mission.' They go further to suggest that New Labour policies have promoted

> the head as the trained and licensed reform implementer embroidered as transformational leader. While there has been a reworking of collegiality as team work, the growth of a leadership cadre in schools has done little to challenge the privileging of head teachers as school leaders, and at most it has generated an oligarchy delegated to deliver the vision and mission.
>
> (ibid.: 169)

The role of support staff

Over the past decades there has been a major growth in the number and use of support staff working in educational contexts to almost half of the school workforce, with a quarter being TAs (DCSF 2009). A large majority of TAs support learners with learning and behavioural needs and thus they are perceived to contribute to the potential of a school to be fully inclusive.

Frameworks for continuing professional development have emerged to provide TAs with the necessary qualifications to demonstrate their understanding of children's learning needs and build their confidence, and in some cases enable them to progress into a career in teaching. When a study on teachers' workload was published (PricewaterhouseCoopers 2001), the remodelling of the workforce (DfES 2002) resulted in the preferred government solution for TAs to be encouraged to take on greater teaching roles and cover non-contact time for teachers engaged in planning, preparation and assessment. This aimed to enhance the TAs' role to cover a wide range of support including pedagogical, pastoral, physical care and behaviour management in a number of different contexts – the classroom, the playground and other locations in the school. The necessity for good teamwork and collaboration between teachers and assistants enabling time to talk and share insights is essential, and Vincett *et al.* provide a useful book of resources and materials to support effective collaboration between TAs and teachers (Vincett *et al.* 2005).

On the one hand, the contribution of TAs to inclusion of all children has been perceived to be very valuable, as in many cases they 'play the role of connecting and mediating in the classroom and school between different children and between children and teachers and parents' (Howes 2003: 150). As the level of TAs' responsibility grew, the government introduced the Higher Level Teaching Assistant status to enable recognition for their skills (TDA 2003).

LSAs work most closely with the child, and quite often with the family, but have very limited voice, power or capacity to influence the inclusive ethos of a school. They often have low salaries and work on a part-time basis. They consequently will live near to their workplace and have a deeper understanding of the backgrounds of the children in the school than the teachers themselves. This insight can be particularly beneficial when learners come from different ethnic backgrounds as their multilingual capacity and understanding of religious and cultural mores are highly beneficial.

On the other hand, a recent large-scale report, 'The Deployment and Impact of Support Staff in Schools' has found that 'TA support has a negative impact on pupils' academic progress, especially pupils with SEN.' The report goes on to state that TAs have 'inadvertently become the primary educators of pupils with SEN' (DCSF 2009).

Webster *et al.* (2010a) go on to say that we need to review the deployment, practice and preparedness of TAs to ensure that those most vulnerable of learners are given the educational support they require. Further reflection on the data reveals that teachers need to be fully engaged in supporting TAs in their work in order for 'students with disabilities to receive equitable opportunities, effective instruction, and appropriate supports in inclusive schools' (Giangreco 2010: 345; Webster *et al.* 2010b). This study is particularly important as it highlights the lack of contribution of TAs and LSAs in relation to children's academic outcomes. In stark contrast, a large proportion of the SEN budget spending of £4.9 billion in 2007–8 was allocated to the recruitment of TAs. The researchers question the use and deployment of TAs/LSAs but fail to ask the bigger question of whether a model of inclusion in education relying heavily on additional adults is a working model.

The role of the voluntary and community sector

The voluntary and community sector has been through changes in its role and status in relation to public sector organisations over the last twenty years. As the Labour government came to power in 1997, it built a compact with the voluntary sector to bring about changes in public sector practices, particularly for services for children and young people. The government provided additional funding for Sure Start (1999) early years provision, which had to include contributions from education, social services, health and voluntary sectors. The voice of the voluntary and community sector has been valuable in broadening understanding of specific needs of local communities and enabling their direct involvement in such provision. The involvement of larger voluntary sector organisations – Barnardo's, the Children's Society – has had a great impact on public services for children and also the emergence of new small voluntary organisations which have supported vulnerable children and families.

A direct way in which this sector has impact on school communities is in consultation processes with children and their families, and subsequent provision of activities such as breakfast clubs and after-school clubs. They are also influential through involvement in governing bodies. A small-scale study in three disadvantaged localities (Dean *et al.* 2007) found that governing bodies can make a valuable contribution to the development of schools; however, in the case study areas they also found that there were difficulties in keeping governors with the time and expertise for the complex tasks involved.

The role of the governor of a school is directly answerable to parents and the community. On the one hand their main areas of responsibility are linked to standards, accountability and strategic development, but on the other, also, involvement in the social aspects of the school community.

The role of the educational psychologist

The role of the educational psychologist has become central in defining educational provision for learners with SEN and disabilities. In the 1970s and

1980s they were primarily concerned with psychometric assessment, drawing together the statement of educational need and clarifying teaching and learning approaches for such learners within an appropriate environment. Hence, they operated as gatekeepers over school placements through their overall responsibility for assessment, identification and the creation of statements. This gatekeeping role continued throughout the 1990s and 2000s, whilst some also focused on curriculum development, supporting teachers to differentiate their teaching and learning approaches, and supporting parents to achieve their goals for their children. More recently, government policy has tried to encourage them to take an active role in school development towards inclusion. This has put educational psychologists in a position where they have to work closely with the child and the family, but also with teachers and school leaders in an effort to effect educational change for inclusion. Within this role they seem to have assumed some power but in a variable and inconsistent way, to a great extent depending on how this role is regulated by the school and the local authority.

The educational psychologist has a very wide ranging and demanding role yet recently the 'move away from individual casework has led to an under-achieving and under-confident profession in danger of becoming obsolete' (Boyle and Lauchlan 2009: 72).

With a reduction in ground-level interventions, several national reports have emerged on the role of the educational psychologist. The Department for Education and Employment (DfEE) Report (2000) and the Currie Report (Scottish Executive 2002) defined very similar core functions for the EP: assessment, intervention, consultation, training and research to be delivered at three levels: the individual child/family, the school and the local authority. The government commissioned a further review (Farrell *et al.* 2006) after the Every Child Matters agenda was introduced, which clarified that the EP would work in the following areas – early years work, work with schools, multi-agency work – and this would be achieved at four levels: the individual child, groups of children, the school and the local authority.

This breadth of engagement has the potential to enable the EP to use individual cases to inform policy makers and bring about change at the local authority level, but how is the training process for educational psychologists preparing them for this broad ranging responsibility for inclusion within any school community?

The role of the social worker

Social workers are trained to degree level to help adults and children to stay safe and in control of their lives, particularly when they are in challenging situations. Social workers' role is to 'make life better for people in crisis who are struggling to cope, feel alone and cannot sort out their problems unaided' (Social Work Task Force (SWTF) 2009). They may work in a variety of settings and organisations, statutory and independent, but their core work is to ensure the safety of all children, particularly the most vulnerable. Their work with families is to assess and manage personal relationships, making judgements and exercising powers when they deem children or adults to be at risk of serious harm. This work is demanding and requires strong interpersonal skills and abilities, 'informed by relevant knowledge and research including child development and attachment; understanding human growth and development; the impact of social and environmental factors; understanding how to respond to manipulative behaviours; and understanding what enables people to fulfil their potential' (Children's, Workforce Development Council (CWDC) 2009).

There is currently a major shortage of social workers in the UK, particularly for work with children due to the demanding work in protecting children from serious harm and the frequently negative perception that society holds of social work.

In 2002 the qualification for social workers became a full degree, and the practical professional skills were emphasised alongside academic insight into the law, partnership working, communication skills, assessment, planning, intervention and review, human growth, development, mental health and disability (Department of Health (DoH) 2002). Since then, following the high profile deaths of children Victoria Climbie and Baby Peter, there have been several research reports. Recently they seek to clarify the role of the social worker, enhance recruitment and retention to the profession and support social workers in the challenging work they do for children, young people and their families (DfE 2011a; Munro 2011; SWTF 2009).

Munro looks at improving the practice of social workers by acknowledging that 'Good social work practice requires forming a relationship with the child and family and using professional reasoning to judge how best to work with parents. Social workers need to make best use of evidence on how to help families change' (Munro 2011: 11–12). Higher education institutions are currently required to review their training programmes to ensure that emerging social workers are prepared for the challenges faced within their professional role. It is unclear how they might construct their contribution to inclusive school communities. Baginsky (2008) writes about the central role of schools in safeguarding all children, with particular concern for those with disabilities, exploring provision in both Scotland and Australia with differing roles for social workers.

The role of the health practitioner

The health service is a vast system of professionals with different areas of expertise, many of whom work directly with children and young people who are of compulsory school age. The Department of Health issued a set of eleven standards as the National Service Framework (DoH 2004) demonstrating their role within the Every Child Matters agenda (DfES 2004). The first five standards have been identified in relation to children and young people as: promoting health and well-being, identifying needs and intervening early; supporting parents or carers; child, young person and family centred services; growing up into adulthood; and safeguarding and promoting the welfare of children and young people.

There are separate documents that clarify the additional six standards in relation to those who are ill, in hospital, are disabled, require support for emotional well-being and mental health, require medicines and/or maternity support. In some locations, health services have been developed through extended school/children's centre contexts to enable all children and young people easier access. The range of health services might include monitoring of obesity, immunisation, family learning, healthy eating clubs, speech and language therapy, counselling provision, smoking cessation and sexual health advice.

The current government aims to 'simplify the system' in order to enable easier access for children and young people to health services but recognises that this will require 'close co-operation between the NHS and schools, with professionals from health and education co-operating in understanding a child's overall needs and their role in meeting them, within a system organised to achieve this end' (DoH 2010: 2.18). This policy guidance document makes considerable mention of the role of schools in addressing mental health concerns of children and young people following a review of the Child and Adolescent Mental Health Services (CAMHS).

The health service has been developing insight to inclusive provision across the range of health practitioners for a long time. The links into educational settings are building through school nurses and speech and language therapists, whose offers of training programmes for schools are almost exclusively taken up by TAs and LSAs. These aim to put in place individual programmes set up by health practitioners.

Health practitioners supporting children and young people with chronic illness or physical disabilities reported that an inclusive and supportive ethos in a school made communication processes easier and led to teachers being 'proactive in other ways such as persuading skeptical colleagues to follow advice from health staff, monitoring children's health-related progress and approaching health staff to ask for advice and training' (Mukherjee *et al.* 2001: 25).

The context for inclusive school communities

Policy guidance for public services working with children, young people and their families throughout the later stages of Labour governance resulted in an overall agenda for cohesive integrated services entitled Every Child Matters (DfES 2004), and five clear outcomes were stated to ensure that children are healthy, safe, that they enjoy and achieve, make a positive contribution and achieve economic wellbeing. This was in response to the UNCRC national UK monitoring process (Tarr 2009), which consistently reported that more integrated services for children were required. Such overall aims became the start of a common language for the different public and private sector agencies to work together for children, young people and their families.

The Children Act (2004) made legislative changes to bring the systems and structures of education and social care departments into closer working partnerships, stating that all agencies had a 'duty to cooperate' for the benefit of children, young people and their families. The Common Assessment Framework (CWDC 2005) was developed as a tool to bring diverse professionals together with children and families to clarify common areas for effective support and provision which reach across disciplinary boundaries. A further document supporting the development of integrated professional training is the 'Common Core of Skills and Knowledge' (CWDC 2010) outlining six key areas – effective communication and engagement with children and their families, understanding of child development, of safeguarding, capacity to support transitions, multi-agency working and the sharing of information.

These policy documents have supported the development of some more integrated training processes for professionals that recognise the need for each discipline to have some insight to those working alongside them. The experience of economic recession, the subsequent retrenchment of different agencies and uncertainties brought about by political changes have created trends against the overall goal to work in partnership. The coalition government in the UK recently attempted to remove the 'duty to cooperate with other agencies' from the school agenda, but campaigners succeeded in maintaining this aspect of the Children Act (2004) to support the most disadvantaged children, young people and their families.

The stories presented in this text span the context of these policy developments and demonstrate the lived experience of this context through the expressed personalised perspectives. Each perspective has a part to play in the education and learning of our children and young people. This text seeks to shed some insight into the different individual voices within the debate to enable each to understand the other and work together with deeper awareness to achieve more inclusive school communities.

Chapter 2

Stories

THE STORIES OF MOTHERS AND YOUNG PEOPLE

Jenny, mother of Ben

'My son Ben has been diagnosed with autism in the first few years of his life. We lived in China at the time and decided to return to England in the hope that we will be able to secure better support for him. In England we managed to organise a twenty-hours-a-week home-based applied behavioural analysis [ABA] programme. Ben did this from the age of four through until the age of eight. Approximately until then he went to his local primary school along with his sibling.

'Before the end of primary school we had to move him to a special out-of-authority provision because he was not coping well in his school. Not long after this he was expelled from the special school on the grounds of his anxiety and unmanageable behaviour. Ben spent some time at home receiving home education consisting of two to three hours a week input from local educational services. He was then placed in another special school, from which he was expelled again because of behavioural problems. By this time Ben picked a few more additional diagnoses ranging from ADHD [attention deficit hyperactivity disorder], to generalised anxiety disorder and most recently bipolar disorder. Again, after some time of home education we finally managed to find him a place in a rural provision for young people with autism, focusing on life skills and aiming to enable him to go part time to a local college doing a course in animal care. So Ben is currently there. We have been in touch with the Children and Young People Service, which provides his daily support, and with the Educational Psychology Service, which is part of them. We have also been in touch with Social Services, which provide direct payments for my own respite, and with Child and Adolescent Mental Health Support Services (CAMHS).

'To me, inclusion means being educated alongside neuro-typical children with lots of adaptations made so that the child with difference can fit in. It shouldn't be that the child with differences has to behave like neuro-typical children; it should be that education should fit this child with his differences.

'If I have to give an example of when he was most included from his school days it would be from his mainstream primary school where the parents of the children in his class were very good at trying to include him out of school, which is a strange example to use maybe, but the out-of-school life has been possibly more important than the in-school life. And certainly, when he was young, in that particular school, and this is not typical of other children's experiences, he was invited to all the birthday parties, and that was hugely important. It dropped away as he got older, but that to me was an inclusive thing. Also, for a while he was a part of the choir there and that particular music teacher who came from outside the school, who had a slightly different attitude, was very flexible and tried to make him a part of it and appreciated what he could get from the effort that he made. In a way perhaps the school in that respect was good in what it was providing.

'I think the big difference is, when he went to special school, on both occasions he was in a residential school. At the time he went, he was not able really to have any friendships with neuro-typical children any more. Friendships have changed at this age to be something different that he could not be part of. When he was in the special school he was no longer on the outside, at least initially; he was no longer in the corridor, which is what school life had become in the mainstream environment. He was absolutely the child on his own, different from everyone. They were fond of him but he was different, and in every way he appeared different. While in the special school, for a time he was one of everyone else. He still managed to get anxious there eventually, and to put himself in the corridor there too, but for a while that was the difference.

'There are a lot of things that make inclusion difficult. For autism, I think the architecture of the school makes it also difficult. If you have got a school with lots of echoing places, lots of children bumping into each other in corridors, large numbers of children made to sit together at assembly for long periods of time; teachers who make children sit on the carpet without moving for too long – those are really difficult. Schools that don't have lots of little rooms where you can go away in groups are a problem. If the architecture of the school doesn't lead to that, or if the head teacher does not use the additional rooms in that way so that the children have to stay in the classroom whether or not they can cope with that – that is a problem; or if you have a school that is not prepared to set up desks separately in the classroom so that they can have independent work stations when the child needs it – that is a problem. Schools that understand the role of visual supports around the school, in the classroom and in teaching, do better. It is also dependent on the attitude of the head teacher. If you have a head teacher who is determined to control behaviour in a sort of boot camp/zero tolerance way then that really doesn't work with a lot of our children. With people who will not make exceptions for differences in some children, on the grounds that if they do it for some they have to do it for everyone, I think you can have a problem.

'For Ben, inclusion has decreased year on year. So the most included years of his life were probably when he was young and was still relatively happy – the ages between about five and eight, and then after that he found the world more and more difficult and has been increasingly unhappy and withdrawn from groups of people. The more he has become aware that he is different, the more he is aware that he cannot manage people of his own age. So I suppose with the arrival of self-awareness, inclusiveness has somewhat decreased.

'It could have been better than it was, it could definitely been better than it was, but whether the end result wouldn't have been the same it is difficult to say. In three different settings he has managed to withdraw from taking part in the group from each setting so maybe that would have been the same no matter where.

'I see my role for inclusion as a politician battling for his rights at all times. Perhaps this was the main difference between the mainstream and the special school. At special school you felt that the school was with you and at mainstream you felt that you are battling constantly against their "He is not the only child here" response. It felt adversarial but hugely painful. I still feel deeply hurt inside.

'I suppose as a child with SEN [special educational needs], a child with autism, he has the right to an education, which means that he can have a school place, where some decades ago he wouldn't have had a school place at all. Apart from this, our journey has been a battle all along: plotting and scheming, and an enormous lot of talking to other parents to find out the best route through things knowing that you will be battled from the point of view of the budget at every turn. I nearly went to tribunal with the application to do ABA when he was small, but the Council gave it at the eleventh hour. We got what we wanted but we got it because we were going to tribunal.

'I run a local branch of the National Autistic Society [NAS] so I help parents in my local borough. It is really essential to help people with inclusive education just because of the numbers. We have now over fifty in each school year and there are probably less than ten places in special schools in each year, so it is a matter of numbers that the vast majority will end up in mainstream schools, whether or not that is the ideal placement for them. So you have to work to make it as good as it can be. And for some it is a very successful place and for others it is not.

'In this borough we have quite a large autism team who spend their lives going to school and trying to educate people in the schools so they made a lot of difference. I don't know if they can catch up really but this has certainly been a step in the right direction. And now the current financial cuts will impact on these services. The autism team has to be reduced by half.'

Ben's story

'First, teachers were teaching me how to communicate easily, now people are teaching me how to achieve independence. I had to spend my life learning just how to communicate, not English, Maths and Science ever, but I was learning how to communicate until I was about ten. Ever since then, or ever since a few years ago and up until now fifteen, and continuing, I have been trying to learn how to be independent but I have been unsuccessful. I think it is . . . because I think a lot of children start learning from about five how to be independent.'

Ben shares his perspective on his education in the schools he visited and how he perceived his experience to be related to (in)exclusion:

'This is about SJ [local mainstream primary] school first, ok . . . In SJ life was so easy, friendships were so easy. Everything, everything that I always did in SJ was learning, education and entertainment – always very, very easy in life, all that, until I was in Year 4. This is when life started to be really, really tough. It was just a dramatic change – life was easy and then life was hard. And now I feel excluded from other people. Well, I don't mean expelled . . . well technically . . . in another school, yeah, because . . . you know when I went to SL [first special school], you know after SJ school . . . SJ school wasn't the right school for me, you know Jenny [Ben's mother] put me in SL and then I was so upset, I was very sad, and they wouldn't expel me, and I would do anything to get out of it. They kept restraining me, they kept locking me in my room . . . it is true, you know, they were evil, evil, evil staff members. Yes, SL, you know . . . it was worse than SJ. They kept locking me in my room and I would do anything to get out . . . so I used to piss and shit on the carpet . . . I never pissed and shitted on the carpet in SJ because MB [the head teacher] would have hit and shouted at me so loudly that I . . . this would have expelled me for life in SJ; but at SL I tried to get expelled anyway because that was really an evil school.

'Then I went to HH special school. In HH school, they had so much security . . . that I would do anything to get out of it. First, I tried to like it, and after that . . . I really hated it, and I couldn't help hating it. And I was so anxious, much more anxious than I was in SL. HT and BT [members of staff] were so evil and invincible that they were just like the Daleks in "Doctor Who", do you . . . does anybody have an idea how the Daleks from "Doctor Who" are invincible? Humans, can you even imagine that the human race can be so invincible! Do you watch "Doctor Who"? Because the humans in "Doctor Who" find that the Daleks are bullet-proof and the humans are not, but apparently TC [member of staff] was very bullet-proof to me . . . or at least he was punch-proof, at least.'

Ben says he felt mostly included in his time at his local primary school. The critical example he shares is when he played a game with his classmates at break time. The game was 'duck, duck, goose' and Ben makes some associations:

'We used to play duck, duck, goose! I remember watching Simpsons the other day, when Ralf kept going patting everyone on the head saying "duck,

duck, duck, duck . . ." Bart was having a very boring party with everyone where Ralf went "duck, duck, duck, duck" without saying "goose" but I was sensible when I was little and I said "goose"; but above all, Simpsons is just fun, eh? Yes, do you remember when somebody used to do cow, pig, horse and sheep and that, and I used to do that as a joke unlike Ralf, who went endlessly "duck . . ." without saying "goose." '

Ben accepts a question about how he thinks the government is trying to help young people like him. This is what he has to say:

'They are not trying to help me, I hate the government, they are my arch enemy actually . . . the government is my ultimate enemy ever, I can't imagine any villain in fiction more evil than the government, who happen to be in the real world itself. I will tell you why the government is so bad to me . . . because they make life depend on finance, unlike in nature. You can just hunt your own food and get food any time you want but with the government, you have to buy food, you have to buy everything, you cannot get something for nothing, but in nature . . . nature's balance is that you can get anything you want at any time . . . I don't want to be included with people. I want to be with the animals in nature . . . I want to live in the wilderness altogether when I grow up. Life will be much more simple if I live in the wilderness.'

Alice, mother of Cher and Adam

'I have two children – Cher and Adam. Adam is severely autistic and Cher is mildly autistic. She is verbal and doing all right in mainstream school. Adam is currently in a special school, which is an ABA school. They are both twelve years old and about to transfer to secondary education. We started them in education a year late because they did their ABA programmes at home, in the hope that we might prepare them better for school, to help them make a bit more progress. I have been involved with children's services since they were born. First it was with Health in relation to developmental assessments and, once they did not pass the second-year test, it was then psychological assessment and all that; then it was the ABA programme which has been running throughout. With Health I had a fight for Cher in trying to get her diagnosed because of her lung problems. It was a complicated unusual lung condition, I suppose, but it took them about five years to realise that it was her lungs. And then the whole fight with Education about special needs in order to try and have their needs met.

'With Education there has been a fight for both of my children initially to obtain funding for their home-based ABA programmes. Then a fight for Adam to go to the ABA school, the school I wanted him to go to. Going to M special school where they wanted him to go would have been hopeless and this is why it was extremely important that he could go to the right type of school. In M school he was in a class of six. Four were verbal and Adam and one more boy were not. When it came to Maths, the teacher said "take them both to soft play because they will not get anything out of this". I kept him there only for a month. In this school all the things he wanted were locked up in cabinets and inaccessible, and he was used to ABA, you know, where if he communicated and asked nicely he should be able to get these things, earn them in some way – not have them locked up and not being able to get them. He had a lot of tantrums because of that and I found it hopeless and took him away.

'It was a question he either went to the ABA school or I set up my own school and in the end, I resigned my own teaching post in order to set up a school but then he was offered a place at the ABA school. So, you know, it is better because it suits him the way we worked with him but also, it is not education to say he can go to soft play, appalling really. The special school doesn't necessarily suit the needs of every child. They meet the needs of lots of children but at that time I think the non-verbal children needed one-to-one.

'With Cher it was mainstream education from the beginning. It is always a battle about hours, and how much supervision she can have and, especially with moving to secondary, it is a battle all over again, really, so it isn't easy. I don't know if it is easy for Cher in the mainstream school. It is very difficult to decide if special education is not the easier route. In the high functioning special school, like the one I recently visited, there are a lot of similar kids, who are doing the curriculum, but they are autistic and have certain learning problems. There she would be a big fish in a small sea, whereas here I am putting her into a very good school, where the pressures on her are much greater, and obviously, in trying to keep up with peer pressure, it may make her feel that she is some inferior being in her heart.

'To me, inclusive education means children with special needs being included in mainstream schools alongside their neuro-typical peers. I don't know how far you are taking it, fully included I presume. I suppose in her primary school Cher had been included in most of the activities that they had, but only to a certain extent. She was included in normal classes, provided her behaviour was acceptable. If her behaviour was unacceptable she would be sent out of the class, which I would say is to be excluded in a limited sense and pointed out as different to her peers. This puts her acceptability to her peers in jeopardy. It is never a 100 per cent any form of inclusion in my opinion.

'I suppose, the moments that stand out for me are when Cher was participating in school plays and productions, which she has done, and singing. I have to say, when I saw her for the first time standing up there (something I never did much of myself, it wasn't my thing when I was in school), that sort of amazed me – that she could participate, learn lines and could sing along with the other kids, yes, that was quite amazing.

'On the other hand, she wasn't allowed to participate in the football team, which I suppose she would have loved to have done and her ball skills are actually quite good, but they didn't even consider her. This was not to do with her autism but with her lung problem, because they felt she wouldn't cope. Yet they allowed an asthmatic child to be in the football team, and this always upset her because she was the only girl left behind when they went to away matches. So I think there are problems with so-called inclusion, where children are actually hurt more in a sense, when they are included in mainstream, because there will always be situations where they are excluded.

'The help that she has, the teaching assistant [TA] that she will have is absolutely crucial and it is of great concern that they may not be up to the mark. I am supposed to have an influence over who supports my child, according to her Statement [of Educational Need], but I haven't had, because of the way the school run their recruitment. In Cher's Statement, TAs are supposed to be recruited jointly with parents and they weren't, of course; the school chose them. They conceded that the TAs could go on courses, because they haven't been trained in ABA and they have to be – it is on her Statement. So we arranged for the two different TAs to go on shadowing courses and I actually paid for it myself. I am concerned, because somebody needs to be able to handle Cher's behaviour in order for her to be included. In secondary [school] it is even more important, because TAs need to under-stand all the subjects, really through to and including the sixth form. If they are not up to it they will be not much of a help to her. Also, just as important for children with autism, if not more so, is help with communication and social skills, but the TA does not see this as within their remit. They are there to help with the academics, whether they are needed for that or not. If not they can help other children, but this does not help the child with the Statement.

'For Adam it is very different because, of course, the special school runs along ABA lines. I feel, in a sense, that they have taken over that side of it during the day. But, of course, I have to meet with the school, and I need to see what he is doing. By the same token, they have to see what we are doing at home and how we are doing things. I communicate with them on a daily basis via his file. This I find a lot easier and less problematic.

'The ABA school where Adam goes would be exclusive in a sense, from neuro-typical children, although they do reverse inclusion, where some children go there, on a drop-in sort of basis, slowly increasing. They come to visit the special school but not in the classroom, in particular. He does not visit mainstream schools, although more verbal children in the school do attend local mainstream schools on a part-time basis and with a shadow or tutor from the ABA school. For Adam, he has in his class other children that are more verbal and I think they provide a good peer situation for him. So I feel he can benefit more from that than from mainstream children coming into the school. I obviously think he benefits from Cher as well.

'In the past I have been able to choose the learning support assistants (LSAs) or shadows for Cher, and her tutors at home who would help her.

'I see my role as one of helping Cher and Adam to cope with their condition, their social problems: relating to other kids in school, and to the rest of the world. But at the end of the day, all that you fight for is meeting their needs. Yes, you may not dare ask at tribunal for what you think *is best* for your child; you have to just ask *to meet their needs*. It doesn't seem to me to be terribly just, that it is quite acceptable and even commendable for parents of neuro-typical children to want *the best* for their children and to fight for it. For children with SEN, this is seen as naïve and unjustified.

'I went to a meeting with Brian Lamb, who is looking at SEN and the role that parents play. I discussed with him the lack of power that parents have, in terms of knowing how good a TA is, and also knowing whether their child gets the support hours that they are entitled to according to their statement. I am always fighting for hours. Ultimately, it is money of course. I can argue my point, but what about the parents who cannot face going to tribunal, or don't think they can fight or argue, or even don't know they can fight or argue? Their children will lose out completely, which isn't fair. So that is a concern. Further, who can afford to keep going to tribunals? Every year, at every annual review, the child with SEN can, in theory, have support time taken away. This can be ludicrously expensive. There must be a better way of running the part of education. I know LEAs [Local Education Authorities] are constrained and they have to somehow look across the whole area, primary, secondary and special education. Clearly, funding is a major issue for them.

'It is extremely hard, when you have to battle for everything with regard to education for children with SEN. It is difficult because you are having a hard time just bringing them up and working at home with them. It is far more demanding than bringing up a child without special needs. So to have these fights as well makes life a good deal harder. It is a full time job, it is very difficult.'

Cher's story

Cher is aware that she has difficulties in learning. She identifies Maths, History and Geography as the subjects that pose challenges for her. She has been supported throughout her life by ABA tutors to whom she feels very close and some of whom she calls friends. Cher knows who supports her and that their occupation is 'tutors'. She is also aware that there is a hierarchy of tutors with differential influence on her life. She identifies me as a teacher. When asked how included she felt in the primary schools she visited, Cher shares: 'I was nervous. A bit scared at first. Then I finally met some friends, I had friends there and it was less scary. I felt like I was part of the school, and like everyone else, like I did everything there.' When asked if this was the case in both primary schools, she hesitated, 'Maybe'. Cher states that if she could choose to go back she would go to them again. She has managed to make friends in both schools.

After a pause and a think, Cher says that the experience that comes to her mind when she felt most included is 'when I was a bunny in a performance . . . in C school'. Yet she recalls that there was a problem: 'I didn't have bunny ears, that was the problem . . . but I didn't mind. I had a ponytail. I enjoyed the performance.'

Since I talked to Cher first she has been moved to a special school. At the verification stage she says that she would rather have attended a special school from the start, as she feels she was bullied, even at primary school, by the boys, and at secondary school by various girls.

She does not want to answer any more questions but she offers an image to illustrate her understanding of inclusion. It is a hand print − a symbol of individuality, a symbol of difference.

Figure 2.1 Cher's symbol of inclusion.

Carol, mother of Josephine

'My daughter Josephine has Apert syndrome, which is very rare. She was born with some features on her skull and face, fingers and toes. So from a very early age she had major operations: at the age of four months she had to have an operation on her skull to make room for her brain to grow, and then over the next eighteen months she had a number of operations to her hands to have her fingers separated. She has quite small hands and cannot bend her fingers and this creates some difficulties for her with anything that requires fine motor skills. Her toes haven't been separated and her feet still look a bit different, which can cause problems for her. However, to be completely honest, the biggest issues that she has are with her looking different. This causes a huge amount of problems because people make assumptions.

'Even when she was very small going out in the street and meeting people they would say "isn't she doing well!" even when she hadn't done anything. I think this was instead of "isn't she gorgeous, doesn't she have a lovely smile!". Every child has positive characteristics, things that are lovely and beautiful about them, and one needs to find them. Because of the different reactions Josephine would have with different people, right from when she was a baby, learning how to relate to people became problematic because she could not predict what people's reactions would be.

'Josephine went to two different nurseries, two different primary and two secondary schools. The difference each time was made by the way teachers and staff related to Josephine and their expectations of her. When it has worked, it was due to high expectations and the teachers taking responsibility for Josephine's education. When it hasn't, Josephine ended up being taught by TAs. In addition, she had an awful lot of people coming in to see her all the time because she was seen by specialists in hearing impairment, visual impairment, she was seen by a speech therapist, an occupational therapist was coming for her, all these adults coming in, pulling her out. I think actually this was quite disruptive.

'When Josephine moved up to Year 3 she still couldn't read. There was a lot of bullying during that time and it was very difficult to get to the bottom of it. We moved her at the end of Year 3 to a different school because she was not making any progress academically and she was quite clearly unhappy. Over the summer holiday we ourselves taught Josephine to read and by the time she got to the end of Year 4 she had pretty much caught up with her peers. At the end of primary school the focus was very much on SATs [Standard Assessment Tests] and on academic achievement. Although Josephine had caught up in her reading she was behind in other areas. She didn't make much progress in Year 6 again because the focus wasn't on her: the focus was on the children that get the important SAT results.

'So I think Josephine's experience of primary school has not been that she was included. She was there, she had a lot of support from TAs, and she didn't have much teaching from teachers. Their expectations I think have been very low, academically and socially. At the time she left primary school she did not have the social skills to cope in secondary school. She didn't have the conversational skills that she should have had to communicate with her peers.

'For secondary education, Josephine went to our local school. Very quickly it became obvious that she was becoming invisible and that she was becoming the responsibility of the TA. She didn't get off to a good start and she wasn't making any progress. It was difficult to get a dialogue with the secondary school and to get to the bottom of what was happening despite the fact that Josephine had a key worker. I think the school didn't really know how to make adaptations that would have helped Josephine. They just preferred to use the TA instead of changing the way things were organised.

'One of Josephine's PE lessons provides a good example of this. When they were doing activities in the gym she was quite upset that some of the children had laughed at her feet, because she has quite unusual feet where her toes are fused. I contacted the school about this and was told that it wasn't a problem, in future in PE lessons she could just keep her socks on. Clearly the problem was just Josephine and not that they had to deal with it at all. This was very much how the school viewed her: she was the problem and there was nothing wrong with the way they were organised, or with the school culture. I think this was really the root of the problem. She wasn't going to change and they wouldn't change.

'We moved her to a school that had a unit for children with physical disabilities. Although it wasn't our local school, it was just a bus ride away. That school had the potential to provide an ideal opportunity because it had a special resource base on a mainstream school site, so she could go to as many mainstream lessons as she wanted to. Unfortunately the schools operated very much as two separate schools with two separate head teachers and staff and very different ideologies.

'On the mainstream site the children did not mix or socialise with the children from the resource base, even at social times. The children from the resource base had their lunch earlier and they ate in a separate part of the dining room. The resource base was very much like a special school and it seemed that they felt the children needed a special sort of care and attention. The children were viewed as different, more fragile, in need of looking after. They were discouraged from having mainstream lessons, and by the time Josephine was in Year 11 and taking her GCSEs [General Certificates of Secondary Education] there was one other child who did GCSE, and this was in Maths only. The resource base tried to protect their children and people felt terribly sorry for them. They probably thought "they are never going to achieve much in life anyway, so we have to make sure they are kept happy".

'Throughout Josephine's education we had to be far more involved than I would have liked to be. I felt like I was always monitoring, watching and checking, complaining and sort of policing Josephine's education. It was very tiring. It was actually exhausting to be constantly monitoring what is happening at school. I think quite often people would get cross and irritated that I was interfering with what they were doing. I didn't feel like I was working together with staff and that it was a partnership, which would have been much more productive. I was fire fighting, when I was hearing things and checking up on things, monitoring and demanding things. Although we tried to avoid making Josephine do extra work at home, there were times when this was unavoidable, if she was to be successful. She managed nine GCSEs in the end. She wouldn't have been where she is now; she wouldn't have been as included as she is now if we hadn't done what we did. It was important to show her that she can achieve and that she can choose what she wants to do and that she has the potential to do well in anything that she wants to achieve.

'So to me inclusion means to be a part of the group that you are in; to feel that you are a valued member of that group; that you are equal although you are different; that you might need more help than others and that you might have things adapted and changed but that you are equally valued and that you have equal rights; and that you have the right to make demands. It means to have the right to have expectations of others without feeling that you are a problem and trouble, and a nuisance. I think a big part is to be socially included, to feel equal amongst one's peers.

'I have very mixed feeling about the "statementing" process and the labelling of children. I am not quite sure how helpful that is. It makes them more different in a negative way. When children are labelled as a bundle of problems then disability becomes a problem and you see the disability rather than the child. And I really think this is actually very problematic. Josephine had so many different labels attached to her. It is easy to forget that it is a real person that you are dealing with.

'A good example of inclusion is from the college where she is now. I think she is very well included there. I think this is because the whole staff took it on board as a team right from the start. They tried to understand her difficulties and they shared their understanding. Together they have decided what they all are going to be doing. They also clearly talked about her social inclusion and use of support staff.

'She has someone to help her in most classes because she writes quite slowly and cannot copy things from the board so people write for her any notes that are necessary. The big difference is that the teachers see themselves as *her* teachers whilst the TA is there to support her. Josephine feels equally entitled to be helped by the teacher as anybody else – it is the first time that has happened for her, really. When they are in the classroom the TA sets herself apart, allowing Josephine to be part of the group, allowing her to chat with people and feel that she is able to do the same as anybody else. If they do any group work the TA steps aside completely because she doesn't need anybody there anyway. I think her role is much more clearly defined for Josephine. I think this is very important because Josephine can now ask if she needs particular help; rather than just having someone to be there prodding her and reminding her, she is now in control of her situation and has that independence.

'At college they did lots of activities at the beginning of the course to create opportunities for the new students to get to know each other and to build some sort of friendship before getting down to working.

'There is also an example of good practice from Josephine's school time; I didn't think I said that but I would like to. In secondary school she had a Maths teacher who did not want Josephine to have a TA in the classroom because she saw the TA as a barrier to Josephine becoming part of the group, working with others and doing paired work. The key difference was that she would talk to Josephine about what she needed and checked with her if she could see the board. The only time she used a TA was when she used textbooks and needed worksheets photocopied in preparation, or she would want the TA to type them out if the quality of photocopying wasn't good. She wanted to build a relationship with Josephine, just like she did with the others in the class, and for Josephine to say if she needed something louder, or if she needed something repeated to her, if she couldn't read what was written on the board, and that was part of Josephine's inclusion. Also, it was enabling her to have those conversations that are about *Eastenders* or about the things they did at the weekend. It has nothing to do with the lesson but nevertheless it is an important part of being in a social group.

'In terms of government policies in relation to inclusion, I think a lot of the policies are there. The problem is how they are implemented and how they are interpreted. Schools create their practices. I think schools' culture and ethos are more important.'

Josephine's story

'For me, inclusion is when everybody is included together, no one is left out, everybody has a part in daily life. In college it is very hard for me to be included in class and in class work but I have friends and I don't feel left out. Not much at the special school . . . it was a separate school . . . they kept us in the unit and wouldn't let us mix with anybody from the main-stream. It started off with being in the special school but with some of the time in the main school. I felt isolated. To have felt included I would have wanted to be part of the group and not coming for lunch from the special school and taken back to the unit. When I was in the mainstream I had a TA so it was very isolating and nobody could get involved. It felt ok to be taught by a TA but I wanted to be part of the class. I didn't make that many friends at that time but I made one friend and it was difficult to see her. We were in different places and I couldn't work with her. We stayed in touch for two years.

'Most time in primary school . . . I was more included in class and outside class. Once, I went on a school trip and the TA let me go with my friend. I felt included in that. We went and had a look at the shops and looked around and talked.

'Another year that was good was Year 10. I managed to find a friend in that year and we are still friends. Also, I had a Maths teacher that tried to find ways of making me included in the class and she told the TA that I had to go to do other stuff and a couple of times she did not know what to do because I had a friend . . . I had someone sat where she was. She did not know what to do . . . but eventually the teacher got her out of the class and it was much better.

'I felt mostly excluded throughout secondary school. I was in "the base" and I couldn't be in any of the groups when I went to the main school. The teachers in the base taught us at a low level. At a higher level is better. You learn more. I had friends in the base but I was the only one who went to the main school. From that time I am most proud that the Maths teacher wanted me included.

'What I learnt in my education is to want to be out there and try to be more included with other people. The hardest thing which I managed to succeed in is to be more confident. At college where I am now there is no problem with working with my friends, I have lunch with them. I work with people in a group and in pairs. Now I really enjoy it. My role in inclusion is that I make sure that it happens; that I take part in group discussions. I work with a charity as well. Yes, I am included in that to make it better for people with disfigurements . . . and for young people out and about. I go to meetings and residential and talk with different people there. I know about the Disability Rights Act. It supports people in what they need . . . their rights and their work, and their education.'

TEACHERS' STORIES

Lucy, primary school teacher

'I've been a teacher for five years in a suburban primary school. I teach Year 5 and I am a Key Stage 2 leader. Every year I've had children with special needs, from dyslexia and dyspraxia to autism, as well as a little girl with Down's syndrome. So we're quite a white middle-class school but we have quite a range of children. Last year we had quite a lot of children from Morocco in the whole school, actually. So we also have quite a few children whose first language isn't English.

'The reason I went into education is because I had a primary school teacher who had recognised that I was lacking confidence because my twin sister is really very bright. I remember him saying that every child has something to give, everybody has something to offer. My mum's sister had Down's syndrome and she died when she was thirteen. She was actually excluded from her school and seen as a troublemaker. It seems really bizarre now to think that somebody with Down's syndrome can be excluded from school as a troublemaker. That had an effect on my grandad: that my auntie was excluded and totally shouldn't have been, not for bad behaviour, anyway. Maybe she needed more of a specialist education, but to label her "badly behaved" is outrageous really.

'My degree is in Criminology and Sociology. I did my dissertation on the effects of education on the young offenders. It was just glaringly obvious to me that a lot of young offenders are children who have been expelled from primary school, or who have just been ignored because they were badly behaved, or they've been labelled in a certain way. For me it just became so clear that these children have been told that they are rubbish at home, or have a group of friends who have put them down. Whatever their circumstances, what matters to me is that actually in the five hours that they are in my class-room they can do well and achieve and that they feel they have something to offer.

'So, inclusive education for me ultimately means removing the boundaries for all children so they can access education and can further themselves, be the best that they possibly can, whatever they want to be. For me it is about finding out what those children have to give. Inclusive education is not only about these children with special needs or ethnic minorities; it is being inclusive for every single child. Even children just like me, who struggled just because I wasn't as bright as my sister, or children who struggle because maybe they're given a different message from their parents at home and so, really, it is just about trying to remove those boundaries, I think, for all children.

'I think as the class teacher my job is to understand all my children, that every single child has special needs, every single child needs things to be adapted for them; they all have ways in which they learn things that they enjoy. If you have enabled certain children to achieve certain things at some point throughout the year – that is really important. Getting a little bit deeper than just what you see, trying to find their interests, trying to adapt the curriculum, to know that there are parts of the year when children will be interested or uninterested and vice versa.

'I can give you an example from my practice where I think we tried our best to be inclusive. It involves Alice, who is a little girl with Down's syndrome. When she started in our school she wasn't walking, she wasn't talking. She is now supposed to be in Year 5. So she's nine, ten years old but probably working at the mental age of two, two and a half. She has just come out of nappies and is developing speech. I have felt that inclusion in the main-stream school for Alice was amazing. She stayed with her age group. I think that my children now have had an invaluable experience having Alice in their class. I think they're well-rounded children with a much better understanding of children with differences. One of them said "It is really weird: Alice can't speak but I still have a relationship with her". I thought this was wonderful, because they would have never had that experience had Alice not been included in a mainstream school.

'She's always had a full-time learning support assistant [LSA] and then this year the discussion with her parents, LSA and teacher was that Alice was no longer accessing anything that we were doing so she was having to have one-to-one with her LSA all the time, which we felt wasn't including Alice, because she was off with an adult on her own. The discussion was that she would actually join a Year 1 class. Now she has been down with the Year 1 class since September and the differences in how her speech has come along that she's accessing things because they're working at that lower level. For me, I think this is amazing inclusion because we are able to offer that rather than just say she's got to Year 5, now she has to go to special school. 'We can't include her any more'.

'I think to be able actually to offer something else . . . It is getting to the point now where she has just been offered a place in a special school from Year 6 onwards so she can get her secondary place, but I think for us to be able to include Alice and to give her these opportunities is amazing. In a special school she would have been mixing with children who are autistic, with emotional and behavioural difficulties and I think the effects that that could have had on her behaviour would have been massive. Because she now is very affectionate and kind and I think that Down's syndrome children tend to be like that, and to be able to be in a mainstream school, where she can continue to develop that rather than see children who struggle with their behaviour all the time. I think it's been really beneficial for her.

'I think an inclusive school community is about having everybody on the same page: parents, governors, teachers, head teacher, and the kids as well; getting the governors on side, bringing in the money, all the new initiatives;

but also having all the teachers doing the same thing as those children move up the school, as well that we all got the same message, that we are all driven the same way. It is about wanting to move forward. It shouldn't be such a huge task but it ends up being. To be fully inclusive you need to have every parent with the same understanding that we have or teachers with the same understanding that parents have.

'As a teacher I have never felt supported by policy because a lot of good ideas come around government-wise, but I've only been teaching for five years and the curriculum has changed three times. So instead of trying to facilitate teachers to get to know their children better what they are actually doing is they change things constantly so that the teacher's attention then goes onto learning a new curriculum, understanding what you are going to teach, and you don't have time to adapt and improve things.'

Tim, deputy head of an inner-city secondary school

'I started my career as a teacher in 1996 in a fairly middle class school in a small town in the North of England. It had a very white, homogeneous, high-achieving student population. After two years I knew I needed a different challenge and I applied to a school in inner London – a multicultural comprehensive with commitment to inclusion, particularly through supporting students and celebrating diversity. This experience really inspired and defined me. I came to my current school as a behavioural specialist and director of social inclusion. I now oversee professional development and performance management. I line manage Year 11 and sixth form. The school is an inner-city multicultural comprehensive school with roughly thirty per cent Asian, thirty per cent black, thirty per cent white British/Irish and the rest is mixed. I would say we are an inclusive school.

'Reflecting back, there were three things that I would draw out as influential experiences from my early life in relation to inclusive education: exposure to inequality from a young age, parental influence and possibly a religious influence – being exposed to an almost evangelical outreach. In terms of shaping my values and belief in inclusion: when I was at school up until the age of thirteen, fourteen, my behaviour was often poor and at times I was out of control. I had two fixed-term exclusions for stealing and for throwing something at the teacher. I remember one specific time when my mother sat me down in front of the television when there was a programme on a home for young offenders. My mother said "you need to watch this because if you don't sort yourself out you will end up there". I believe this was probably what I call a "trigger point" in my life – a specific experience which brought about change. As a result, I believe I have a strong sense of empathy – I know that students can fail for all sorts of reasons, but there may well be trigger points that are worth working for which can change students' lives for the better.

'When I did my A-levels and I studied the sociology of education, I was blown away, completely blown away by the work of Pierre Bourdieu. He basically argued that educational achievement is not necessarily to do with intelligence but to do with the cultural capital that students enter school with. I just remember looking back at my schooling and thinking how true it was. I think in terms of shaping my values and beliefs in inclusion this was also influential.

'For me, inclusion is about fairness and looking at students and under-standing that they're not all the same, but celebrating this difference and always trying to look at difference in a positive way – disability, sexual orien-tation, ethnicity, family background and many other factors – being positive about these things, celebrating them and not allowing them to turn into a disadvantage for the student. We are not born equal. We are not born with the same opportunities. As an educationalist, as a teacher, as a leader and as a manager I feel a sense of responsibility, it's part of my values, it's part of my vision to make sure that the colleagues I work with and the school as an organisation, do everything to try and give that support that compensates for the disadvantage that some students often have.

'So for me, education is one of the solutions in life in terms of trying to eliminate inequality. It is an opportunity for the student to override the disadvantage that they may have. However, inclusion can be challenging to manage. For me, inclusion is about juggling three balls: it's about first of all supporting the needs of the individual students, but it is also about supporting the needs of other students, a group of students and a class of students. Thirdly, it is about supporting the needs of your staff. If there were enough resources and funding, I believe every student could learn in a mainstream school. There could be extra classrooms, spaces and staff. Staff could work specifi-cally with individual students, or small groups of students, who have complex behavioural and emotional and social difficulties and work hard to integrate them into the student community.

'An example from my practice where I think inclusion has worked comes from the time when I came to my present school. I worked with a student called Robert in Year 8. He was a looked-after child, his mother had mental health issues. So he was in long-term foster care. I worked incredibly hard with him. He was very challenging – his behaviour was disruptive and he would get into confrontations with students and staff. I had him on report with me. I had to work continually, almost like a sort of father figure. I kept on following things through with him, sitting, reviewing and mentoring. When he was leaving at the end of Year 11, I remember him doing a project in Design and Technology. It was a great project and he did a presentation in a school assembly. He was at a high risk of exclusion, and I could see the fruits of my and other teachers' labour who had supported him. Even though he never acknowledged me or thanked me I knew I had had some impact on his success.

'As you become more experienced you become more strategic in student support. I have occasionally seen situations of "professional dependency" of a student on a teacher or professional which I believe needs to be avoided. The problem with professional dependency is that once the professional leaves a school, what then happens to the student? The support therefore needs to come from the organisation and not one individual, although individuals have key roles to play in organisations.

'In our present education system I have learned that you can't afford to be too idealistic about inclusive education. Given the resources available, there are some students that are unfortunately beyond the school remit. A school as an institution is there to develop knowledge and skills; part of this is addressing the social and emotional needs of students. However, it is only part of it and it cannot be main purpose. We work with a whole group of colleagues who come from outside agencies – child and adolescent psychotherapy, counsellors, educational psychologists, police, social workers – but students have complex needs and they can't always be supported by the school. Maybe given more resources this could happen. However, as staff we have a job to do and that is to educate students. We need to try and break down those barriers that we can do but there is a limit. When the impact of one individual is too great on other students or on staff I also have a duty of care to support them. This can mean that you have to make tough decisions which can have an impact on people's lives. These are not nice or easy decisions to make.

'In terms of inclusion as a school community matter, I believe the most important factor is the leadership of the head of the school holding values about inclusion. I think it is crucial that it comes from the head, from the senior leadership team and disseminates down to all managers, staff, students and parents. It's a way of thinking; it's in every policy and should be in every part of the school. It's a philosophy and vision, seeing schools as the place where you can learn and try to correct inequalities. In terms of government policy, I think the Every Child Matters agenda has been brilliant. Education has become more inclusive. However, I have just read the recently published white paper which appears to be moving away from community cohesion. Government cuts can often have an impact on the most vulnerable and I am fearful about the effect these cuts might have on inclusive education. There are, however, some positive parts of the white paper, for example, schools supporting each other, which I believe is good practice.

'In terms of building an inclusive school community, getting parents involved in their son's or daughter's education is very important. If parents connect with the school then they are more likely to support their son or daughter in their learning. For example, we do two things in this school. Firstly, we invite the parent to come in and see their son or daughter participating and being successful, and then secondly we celebrate diversity and culture. It's sort of breaking barriers. It is celebrating their culture, appreciating their culture but most crucially it's getting them into the school.

'I think central to the school is that students should give and contribute to the community – the local, national community and international community. One of the roles of a school leader is to raise awareness about the local community. So at the moment I'm thinking about projects. I am very excited about one project at the moment. I am planning for students to go into a local care home for elderly people and teach residents how to use the Internet. There is a big digital divide between the young and old and young people generally are very much more ICT literate than older people. I believe this project will be good for the students because it will raise awareness and make them feel good about themselves. It will also be good for the residents because it could open up a whole new world to them and make them less isolated from their family, friends and society. Everyone's a winner. Setting a project like this up takes little effort from the manager compared to the impact that it can have on the community and students, but you know it makes life better.'

Bob, retired deputy head of an inner-city secondary school

'I have worked as a teacher and deputy head teacher in two inner-city secondary schools in London for thirty-four years. Throughout my professional experience, to see inclusion as central to the growth of the whole school and to become the focal point of the local community, I have to say it has been quite amazing. Recently I retired but continue to be involved as a consultant in education projects for various local authorities, institutions and organisations, both in the UK and abroad.

'The notion about inclusivity in education is fundamental to everything I did, it was the reason I went to education and became a teacher. As a working-class child I very quickly recognised, in my day in the 1950s, passing an exam – that through passing my 11+ I was selected to go to a very elite grammar school and that gave me an education that absolutely opened doors to professional life. I had an exclusive, elite education and kids that I played with who lived in our street and who were my mates suddenly got selected to go to another school. I felt in my bones that they were at least as intelligent if not more intelligent than me. So suddenly having this experience at eleven made me think that there was something wrong with the system but I passionately desired to go and make my future with my education. So, my experience of a grammar school education made me ironically passionate about the comprehensive system and I am totally and utterly sold to education being a passport to a better life.

'We need to understand education as a lifelong learning process. The modern world requires kids today to make changes in their profession perhaps five times during their lifetime, and often for jobs that have not yet been invented. So being open-minded, being open, having the toolkit in order to respond to changing situations and learn or relearn or learn new things when you need to – that is the whole importance of education and importance of inclusivity to let people access that. Because if you don't, you are going to be one of these "have-nots" even more in the future than is true today. Learning for life, learning for job, learning for change in a rapidly changing world we haven't even begun to realise is changing. The future that today's kids will face will see even more rapid change than we had to deal with.

'You look at policy – government education policy – and you can see clearly that there are strands that promote equality of opportunity through education. So we can demonstrate in law that we are an equal society. The proof of the pudding is in the practice, though, and the practice is patchy because there is no template, there are no things that you compulsorily have to do.

'In my view the notion of equality of opportunity to education is but a small step to inclusivity, really. Inclusion is an all-pervading philosophy for people like me. It means providing an education that is equitable for all and accessible for all, so for those for whom there are barriers to learning, those barriers are as far as possible removed and support systems are put in to help them access what everybody else can access.

'You can talk the talk and make noises about inclusivity and equality and accessing all the good things the school and the curriculum have to offer by their inclusive philosophy but let us not forget that inclusion costs money. And whilst at the sharp end – kids with Statements – there is some sort of acknowledgement of that with some sort of resources, taking it all through to its broadest base – inclusion comes at a cost. You have to find that money and it is incumbent upon the school to go and find these resources or to budget in a particular way that acknowledges what you need to do for your school community in order to have everybody equally participating.

'A school has to have an *efficient* planning process that includes a continuous monitoring to make sure you are meeting the needs of everybody. It is interesting when you look at Ofsted [the Office for Standards in Education, Children's Services and Skills] and what you need to do to be anything other than unsatisfactory – they would expect you to be inclusive. It is not a satisfactory lesson if there is one child in this class who is not learning. So you need to understand your client group, to understand the context in which you are working with them and then start to develop structures to support those groups. You know that is the whole art of management in the school – management of scarce resources in order to meet the spectrum of needs. I suppose this is why schools end up having priority areas each year. And now you would be able to see at my school, which is true of other inner-city schools too, that trend of inclusivity permeating all the thinking that goes on in the school. It is not just a sort of a bolt-on thing. For me the key to inclusivity is to have support and interventions available on site at a school level that enable swift and easy referral at the point of demand. Swift and clear diagnosis of learning problems and difficulties by the school are pre-requisites also.

'First, there is a need to recognise what a community is in the school and wider community; setting up channels and systems of communications and dialogue to understand that; making sure that you are properly understanding barriers to learning, which then gives you the chance to design structures to support that. A proper dialogue with parents is vital. We had a lot of English as an Additional Language [EAL] kids and refugee kids, and asylum-seeking kids. Inevitably those kids come with issues, not just emotional and behavioural issues, but self-esteem issues, confidence issues but also that whole potential exclusivity because of the lack of language. So there is all of the jigsaw puzzle. You got a constantly debated curriculum: what is appropriate for the formal and informal curriculum, and what is appropriate for kids to have for modern living? What do you do to support and challenge your teachers to constantly give that perfect lesson in the way that you train your football team to be as skilful as possible? What are you doing in terms of your money? What are you doing in terms of information and data about families and kids? And all of those are ingredients to provide an inclusive framework.

'I think in Britain, absolutely in Britain, teachers employ the widest definition of their role. I have been to schools in France, Germany and the USA, but I have observed this only in Britain. In France if you aren't teaching you can go out, in secondary teaching you can teach for two lessons and you are out. It would be unheard of; you would be sacked in the UK. So teachers in the UK have a variety of roles: we are deliverers of knowledge and skills-based education, we are social workers, we are youth workers, we are youth offending workers, we are mentors, counsellors, sometimes psychotherapists and substitute parents. That is great in that we more holistically take that on board and do not compartmentalise it, but it is a pity that there is no recognition of that wider role that even an ordinary educator takes on board. I don't think that teachers – particularly primary school teachers – should teach (have contact time) for more than fifty per cent of their working time. Because to do what I have told you – to prepare the perfect lesson, to analyse the data, to liaise with the family and the community, to do the individual work that is often what our kids need – is more than just standing in front of the kids. So recognise this reality and give the teachers the means to do the job – this is what I would say. Our unions should have taken this up as a task for action rather than just focusing on pay. I fear our time to fight this fight is now passed and in these economic times our broad definition of our role as teachers seems now crystallised.

'I can give you many examples from my professional experience for illustration but one comes clearly to mind. It is about a girl called Winifred:

dopey, not good looking, very emotionally charged, eleven years old. She comes to my school and she is the kind in the class who is always attention seeking, who doesn't have very good concentration levels, who storms out and you have to bring her back and all that, and her reaction to stuff is to walk away. A classic EBD [educational behaviourally disturbed] pupil. We had to do a lot of work with her but through the patience of the teachers, and I have to include myself in that, the girl came around. She survived in education, did not get expelled, she went on to have a life. She didn't necessarily go to university but her education was completed, it shaped her, it's made her buy into education as a tool to move people's life forward. She then went off and disappeared for a couple of years. Ten years later, there is a knock on my door when I am a deputy head teacher of the school, and there is Winifred there sobbing in a way that I remember her when she was an eleven-year-old girl. She has come to beg me to find a place in our school for her son, who had been expelled from another school. She split up with his dad, the kid reacted badly to it, and he is a big boy with learning difficulties, and a lot of the big boys with a learning difficulty end up developing behaviour problems as a mask to the real problem.

'The pattern then is repeating generationally, as it so often does. So Winifred is crying, she is all over the place. When we take him on board she is absolutely delighted. I end up spending more time with him than I did with Winifred. He needed pastoral support, he needed to be on report, he needed to be targeted, he needed the opportunity to talk through and be counselled about the way he was behaving and the way he has been, and this whole thing about him needing to be socialised in the classroom, not only for himself but for everyone else. He needed an adult man figure in his life to draw the line for him. He is a lovely lad; he didn't do particularly well in school but he was provided with education, he has gone on and he is working and having a life now. He is a father and happy and grateful that he completed his education, avoiding exclusion. Now, Winifred is absolutely sold on education because of the way we looked after him and nurtured him and she knew that without the particular attention with the needs he had, this kid wouldn't have survived. You know, there is a massive correlation between education failure and crime.'

Peter, head teacher of a special school

'I did a BEd [Bachelor of Education degree] specialising in History. Then I worked on a summer play scheme in a hospital where they had a health authority school, in the villa with residential accommodation for children with severe learning difficulties [SLD]. This was the first time I had met children with learning disabilities. I was a rebel – a hippy, not interested in conventional approaches. I saw these kids and thought – they are real rebels, they are really free. They were not bound by rules. I came into special education at a time when teachers had to buy reading books and hide them in the cupboards from the head teacher. We tried to teach the children to read – put the books in front of the kids and read them to them until they started to read back. The head thought we were completely wasting the children's time.

'I worked with Drama, Dorothy Heathcote approaches to role play. The curriculum was opening out, becoming exciting. I was the lonely clown, the sad giant, the tramp and I would put soil on my face and lie in the corner in the hall and the kids would come in. They knew it was me but they were using their imagination and they could do it. I was pushing for a very conventional non-rebellious philosophy: a normal approach for these special school children who were in segregated special schools.

'I asked for an interview with the SEN education adviser and he sent me to work in mainstream schools. I worked in a primary school in a low socio-economic area. The advisor was trying to subvert the system as SEN support teachers were teaching children in cupboards: testing kids. He put teachers with experience of special schools to work with the mainstream teachers.

'The primary school teacher said "The children cannot do anything", and I said "Yes they can". I wrote on the blackboard and she said "Your handwriting is appalling; you do not understand letter formation". She taught me how to do it after school in order that I might be able to work in the class. I learned a lot about how to talk with kids and what a primary classroom is like every day. She was impressed with the way I was able to work with the kids who were having difficulties. The culture of the primary school impacted on me, as what you did with pupils really mattered. In the special school in those days it did not really matter – completely crazy – there was a culture of acceptance of anything you did, low standards of expectations. However, in the primary school everything mattered: in the real world expectation is very different. This is where my principles came from and how it formed me.

'I am now head teacher of a school for children with SLD aged three to nineteen years. I have been here for over twelve years. We are in the midst of a major rebuild project: the primary department shares a site with a primary school that was finished in September 2010. We undertook this project with a primary school under the auspices of the local authority because both schools, primary and special, required a rebuild. The authority had the land available.

'The second phase is underway now with the secondary department. Refurbishment and the new building are due to complete in September 2012. The aim is to create a secondary ethos for young people from the special school; we have forty-five pupils in secondary and forty-five pupils in primary – a special school of ninety pupils all together.

'Twelve years ago, when I started as the head teacher I instigated that the teachers from primary schools would join with the special school teachers and assistants and work in a team situation. Children had been going with their

TA in a little bubble to local primary schools. I asked why not the whole class, with all our class staff and their teachers and assistants? I took the model from my experience of working with mainstream teachers.

'When designing it here, today, for mainstream and special school together, we built classes in parallel because it is a massive transition. There are many barriers which come out to hit you when you come out of your special school and have the audacity to raise your head. People prefer when you stay in your special school. Change is hard for people. The barriers are very powerful. You have to build a transition. You can only go at the pace of the people: if you go too far or too fast and tread on them then you can wreck it. Our philosophy is to reduce the expectations. If you lower the expectations then you have time to think and work out the social dynamics, to learn where you are before you rush around doing things.

'The school is a butterfly shape, with a primary wing and a special wing. We gave away some of our space to primary as the financial formulas were different but we made sure that the classrooms were all the same. Primary have small group rooms next to every room for one-to-one and group work, the same as we do in the special school. The ceilings can take ceiling hoists in the mainstream classrooms. The school will be here in eighty or a hundred years so the infrastructure is made to enable an integrated school – we have built a KS1 [Key Stage 1] special school class next to a mainstream class and so on. However, at the moment we have a wing for the primary school and a wing for the special school.

'Unfortunately we have two receptions, two staircases, two staffrooms, and two halls. This is rubbish in terms of inclusion, but if we had not accepted these things the project would have stopped, definitely, so you can only go at the pace that other people can go at. Other people need to learn, there are human fear-based reasons, change disorientation, and all schools are vulnerable to this.

'Paulo Freire's concept in *Pedagogy of the Oppressed* [Freire 1971] applies to both schools, as the primary catchment area is within a disadvantaged socio-economic context. The other schools nearby are very middle class. Primary kids in our partner school are from the local housing estate and they are oppressed. There is a siege mentality. So we sat down and said let's look at it and come together. We are both oppressed, the primary and the special school children, but in different ways. It is a strong political statement to make. Freire says that traditionally, oppressed groups attack each other so we are cautious here: by not attacking each other we are making progress. We are getting on fine, we are talking, and we have "Friendly Fridays" where pupils from both schools play together, it is a start. We put some money together and are building additional play equipment on the hard core play area outside. What you have to have is a "giving philosophy". We gave space, we are giving the equipment away, and we give half the swimming pool away. You have to keep giving and when it does not work you have to give more. Freire thinks this approach, a deep understanding about the reality of oppression, combined with a philosophy of giving, is attractive to both Christians and to Marxists.

'In relation to the secondary part of the school the politics were complex, we forged strong links with a range of secondary schools to stop being in an exclusive environment. We joined a local cluster of secondary schools as a full member of that partnership. It has taken two to three years to establish our position in that partnership and to begin to understand the secondary culture. These secondary schools occupy the catchment areas for our secondary pupils so we have established ourselves with the secondary heads and deputies and further education college, which is important for us.

'Links are established through personal networks to create a range of projects: an opera project with one secondary school – writing an opera together; their students organise our sports day, they teach our pupils the games needed. At another secondary school our pupils go to on a regular basis, they converted a caretaker's bungalow into a learning space and their ASDAN [Award Scheme Development and Accreditation Network] groups work together with our KS3 students in the bungalow. These are exciting projects but underneath this we worked with the secondary school cluster to manoeuvre us into this position. You need locational opportunities with local schools and the local community. You need to link with secondary schools. They usually have the subject expertise. We are working with subject coordinators. The new secondary building has specialist rooms for DT [design and technology], science, music, art and food technology for the first time. Would secondary pupils benefit from this environment? We have got things to offer them – BTEC [Business and Technical Education Council] qualifications in health and social care, for example; we can offer them many real learning opportunities.

'The only way to justify what you do in relation to inclusion is through the learning which takes place, so my definition would be – a learning definition. The reason they should be together is because learning is more effective for all of them when they are. As a deputy head, I took kids to the middle schools and saw better behaviour and more attention. Because the middle school kids were listening to the teacher and behaving, our kids listened because everyone else was. It changed the way they were and they were learning more effec-tively. A lot of peer tutoring [took place] – mainstream kids had to explain things to our kids and when I watched I realised that the mainstream kids had to come to terms with the learning they were doing. So the mainstream child had to think about what they were doing and what they were learning in order to help somebody else do the learning, which is what peer tutoring is about: the self-reflection of the mainstream learner. This was good for our kids. You have a win–win situation.

'Inclusion is an entitlement, it is an equalities issue. Where it is difficult, it is about the teacher's skill of differentiation. If you do not understand the basic core learning outcomes then your differentiation will fail. A teacher needs to be tuned into the subject area. If you are not a subject specialist you are a differentiation specialist, then you are limited by your understanding of the core aspects of the subject you are teaching. You can explore this through lesson observation. I observed a Geography lesson – water play to increase understanding about oceans, but half the kids were just doing Maths. They were measuring with jugs in the water play. This was pure math, not even cross-curricular Maths. If you are teaching Geography about the oceans, about the North and South Poles for example, how would you do it? You need to replicate mini icebergs, mini snow landscapes to be really about Geography. You need to know and then use materials imaginatively to teach this.

'We view the national curriculum as the core of what we do; we want to make our school as ordinary as we can make it. When the national curriculum was instigated we needed to be more imaginative in a special school. We did not teach History in special schools in the 1970s as we did not think it was possible. The model of the curriculum was bizarre in those days, and we did a lot of swimming! Now when we started French and parents asked why? We say "Where did you go on holiday?", someone answers "the Loire", so this is why. Our kids are all over the globe during their holidays, so Geography becomes a vital part of their curriculum.

'We employ teachers from mainstream and newly qualified teachers who are not coming with the old mentality – "Ok, I have to do it in different ways but still do the curriculum." We will soon have an artefact corridor for History, like the History of the World in 100 Objects. We need to take a specialist approach to be meaningful for children with complex learning difficulties; they need concrete experiences but then all children benefit from such approaches. Employing a range of resources and facilities is crucial for our kids, making the curriculum work for them is an essential part of the teaching strategy. We do things like a mainstream school does but adapting it for our kids.

'We took the opportunity to build two schools together, primary and special, and now it is a collective responsibility to take it on further; this creative momentum is advantageous. I have found it important to have reflective time, to stand back and look at it again and understand what has been achieved.'

STORIES FROM SUPPORT STAFF

Robert, learning support assistant in a primary school

'The biggest influence on me in terms of inclusion has been my parents. My mum ran a Brownie group and she opened it to everyone. She had a disabled child in her pack and enjoyed trying to get activities that everyone could do together. I went to Brownies when I was growing up. My dad, his partner in business was a disabled man. I got on very well with his son who did not have disabilities but he was an older role model to me. That has had an influence upon me. Dad was a printer and did a lot of leaflets for a place for adults with learning difficulties; I was interested to know about it.

'My housemate came to my university and studied 'Early Years'. She became a nursery manager and now is working for the NHS. She has been a real inspiration for me and now she often recognises special needs from birth through the early years. She got me my first job at the play scheme which was when I adopted this attitude that play can be inclusive even when there is no educational inclusion. A kid can play in any context; not allowing a kid to join in because of their needs is not right, I am always willing to help them out. I never put up a barrier because that kid cannot speak or is in a wheelchair: they can always join our play scheme. I believe that play is an inclusive process. If you are dealing with "normal" kids, for one kid not to be allowed to join in because the other kids do not want them to, that is not inclusive. For the colour of their skin, their religion; I hate to see kids not playing. It might be because in my past I was not allowed to join in, I do not know.

'I started working in schools and I kept the same attitude, whether that was in the playground or in the classroom. It seems the wrong thing to do to send the kid out of class for being naughty. It is a difficult subject because on one hand you have all the other kids in the class who are missing out on their education for a kid who cannot be bothered or is messing around. Yet on the other hand we have a kid we do not know enough about or we are excluding the whole time. It is a dilemma. An example in terms of SEN is a group of three kids – twins and a girl – always taken out of class, a little group, always the ones taken out, and one of the LSAs had them as her little group. It feels a bit sad – why cannot they be included in class or why cannot every child have the chance to go out in a little group? They were taken out maybe for some additional support as they were a little bit behind. I ask is the teacher doing her best for those kids or is she relying on the LSA to educate them? My current research is about the interventions that are going on, how beneficial are they for those kids for their social development. It is often the same kids taken out for Maths and for literacy interventions, or taken out for different things and they are missing PE or art or something they are good at. I want to explore the real inclusiveness of these interventions.

'My work has been with one kid with a Statement so he has been allocated some of my time. I would only take him out of class to do a bit of reading or comprehension at the start of the day and then we would come back in and I would work with him in Maths and literacy with the whole class. They only wanted me to cover the core subjects. That was good but you are seen as "Ryan's special helper" which is not very nice for him that way. It is a very difficult thing to get right.

'I spoke with an educational psychologist and she said it is not just your job to sit with him and do things; you need to be the one who is organising resources for the whole class to get things ready so that they can all work together. If the teacher has written on the board you could say "do it a bit bigger so Ryan can see it". It is not just going to benefit the child with SEN but the whole class; I think this is a good idea. It is tricky because you only find out what to do in the lesson as it starts. All the kids could be sitting listening to a lesson introduction and I am the spare part, but as the lesson starts they all want help because they do not understand what the teacher said. It can be my job to go over and over again what the teacher said. I know it is my role but should it not be something the teachers are doing to start off with? The usefulness of a child being in mainstream school; is it even the right place for them? In that everyone is sat on the carpet [with the] teacher is saying do this and then do this, "activity 3 and then 4". One kid can be working out what 3 add 4 are. You just feel that the teacher has got a tough job anyway, you do not want to make it harder. Is it benefiting the kid to be in class with everyone? I do question everything rather more now.

'I think we need to sort out the whole education system. The school I am in does not provide education in a way that gives the lower ability children more confidence. The staff attitude is still a rather negative approach. I think because of the job I am doing at the moment I would like to see teachers working with TAs more. There is a lack of communication. It is assumed that taking them out might help them, but as they are the same kids always coming out what is the impact on them? I would like every kid to be heard to read each day – that would be inclusive – no matter what level they are. I guess you need more money into the education system, or different teacher training.

'I am really struggling at the moment to identify my personal belief. I was so sure that inclusion was really important and that it is down to the teachers to set the right work for each kid in the same class, good access to differentiation. My role is to help them in class. I am not so sure now

'When it worked the best was in my first year as a LSA and the teacher was not very organised but I liked her style. I had a group before SATs and it was the ones in the middle, eight kids who needed a bit of extra support to get the next level, really focused, eight-week programme, twice a week. The thing that made the difference was that the teacher and I would talk about the lesson, who was achieving what and she would check their homework. I felt we were working together and she got the chance to work with the lower-ability kids. We understood the difficulties of each other's work. I enjoyed that. When you are left alone it becomes difficult then. The teacher needs to be involved in what I am doing with them. It does not seem like they realise my qualifications, they just accept it. It feels like the teacher is not really bothered about what I do with the kids.

'It is a bit different in the resource base: we are joint partners all working in together, one teacher and two LSAs, which is a one–to-one for three kids, sometimes a few more. We know the kids the same amount, we have time to talk about the kids. The kids might not be able to sit in a class of thirty because of individual issues they have, so they need a smaller, quieter environment. They have a support worker for lunchtimes and assemblies so they have social and locational inclusion but they remain in the small class for lessons, which is a good thing. From the resource base one child got back into mainstream, one went into a special school and the other was going back to mainstream for certain lessons. In terms of SEN we do not want to alienate those kids but need to give them specific help, so we can cater for specific needs.

'For my mainstream work I am with Year 3. I am on duty at lunchtime and morning duty some days so this eliminates any time when the teachers are free to talk to me. I am not given any lesson planning so I just turn up and do what I am told, it is very different. I might feel I have a better understanding of what the teachers are trying to achieve if we had time to talk, generally more teachers and LSAs working together. If I feel more valued by the teachers I can value my work more, and if I value my work more I should be able to deliver higher quality work whether in class or specific interventions. It is down to individuals' and class teachers' attitudes, what is best for the kids and how they work with the LSAs.'

Pat, teaching assistant in a special school

'I went to a Waldorf school as a secondary-aged child, there were lots of different children there and we all learnt to be more accepting of our differences. There were children that were not accepted in mainstream schools, parents had tried many schools and a Woldorf school was more accepting. The ethos there was that we are all equal as human beings, which is my ethos and my parents' too, so that was where it stemmed from. When I was a teenager my cousin got throat cancer and we visited her a lot. I thought what they did in the children's hospital was fantastic. As an adult I volunteered in the children's hospital, only clerical work, evenings and weekends.

'My interest in working with children with special needs was not necessarily one thing, it was all sorts of things. When my own children were at school I did not like it when other mums in the playground would say things about children in the classroom. I would say I am glad they are in my child's class so our children can learn to be accepting, and that is a really good quality that we cannot teach them as parents, and so if they can experience it that is something they will actually learn from experience. Life is like this, we are all different, we have our funny ways, we need to learn to be accepting.

'I set up a playgroup for mums and dads and pre-school children and it was called "Messy Play" to encourage them to do painting, playing in mud, as so much is to be gained from this. We tried to get the traveller community involved in this. I visited them with a social worker. They did come along to a couple of sessions but it was not particularly successful; however, it was a start and began to break down a few of the barriers between the local community and the travellers. We also ran Tumble Tots and we kept five places back for the traveller community. Unfortunately they never attended it but we did try. I used to pick up mums and their babies who could not get out easily from their high-rise flats. The social workers would say there are some families who are hard to reach and would benefit from encouragement. I had a baby too, so I would visit them and I was on an equal footing with them. The Sure Start aim was to reach those families who found it hard and could not afford to come; this was successful. We also ran a gym session for a period of time for all children.

'I did a diploma course in Childcare and Education when my youngest was at playgroup. I did a placement at the children's hospital which I really enjoyed. I had a placement at a special school where I am now. I did enjoy mainstream schools but got a bit bored. I enjoyed the hustle and bustle of special education to keep me on my toes.

'Adults need to stop using generalisations and clichés and concepts and media hype and just stop a minute and listen and try to understand and hear a bit of history from that child, their parent, their teacher. You might see a child presenting challenging behaviour that is only the surface. You would be amazed at their history and then you would think actually that is not too bad. Children are much more accepting than we are, they are very open. If they can experience all different kinds of children from a young age then as they grow up into adults [they] will be less judgemental about one another. We are all very different.

'I agree with segregation of children with really difficult behavioural problems or very physically aggressive children that cannot cope. They have to have that smaller environment with more adults, maybe something less structured or more structured, depending on what is appropriate. But I think it is really important for the mainstream children to accept and experience the special needs children, and the special needs children to accept the mainstream children. Once they leave education there is nothing, they are dropped from a great height, there is nothing there as the funding just stops at eighteen years. All the support just disappears, so they really need support during the school years.

'Some provision can be rather tokenistic, but there are always those dilemmas. Some mainstream schools are really into inclusion because they think their children and their school community will benefit from it in some way. Some of them really do not want inclusion but they have to because it is forced by the government, because it is felt that schools have to be inclusive whether they want to or not. So it is quite personal on the head teachers really, whatever the heads' views are will be the incentives for them. Many adults do not know, they have not had the experiences, they have not seen it before, it is alien to them. Now children are experiencing playing and working together, which will make them more accepting as adults, more understanding with more insight, better people all round.

'In my school we have a main special school site and seven units in mainstream: three are for children with autism, others for children with moderate to severe learning difficulties in both primary and secondary schools. These satellite units have developed as government policy developed towards inclusion, so we set up these units for children. All children have uniforms from the special school and everything is managed from here, inclusion under a very thin banner as it is only slight. Some are included more than others; it depends upon the mainstream school. If they have good relationships, mainstream children will come into the special school classes for English and Maths and they go out for PE. They share playtimes together and lunchtimes in the primary school. In the secondary school they tend to go back to their tutor room. Many do go out to play with a TA with the mainstream classes. It depends how much they share.

'Initially there were some real difficulties bridging this gap between the two schools – mainstream and special – as loads of barriers had to be broken down. There were lots of incentives in place: if you let us come down we will give you a new games room or a computer suite. All right, we do not really want you but we will get some new computers. Actually it was difficult to persuade the mainstream schools that this is the way it is going. The children definitely benefit from going to the mainstream school – they are mixing with other children at playtimes, lunchtimes and some lessons. There is not so much of a stigma which there often is for a child with special needs. The mainstream child is also benefiting which is an important aspect. At one secondary school they had a real problem with physical location: the autistic unit had a segregated playground with corridors outside and balconies above their playground – very badly thought out. The mainstream school children would shout out to the autistic children on the swings horrible names and chuck things at them. This was a big problem: they had lots of assemblies, explained about autism and how it presents itself. It made a difference: the kids, once they understood about autism, they were not calling them weirdoes and freaks, they understood it. There was a big change and they then supported the kids – "Oh, are you alright then?"

'We have got some children of secondary school age in the special school context that should be with mainstream. Young people who do not present with any behavioural problems, they could cope with the social things ok but they are just not academically able so they come back to us, which is a real shame for them. I can think of five young people who were not able to go to mainstream due to academic levels.'

Eva, learning support assistant in a primary school

'Coming to university is the biggest example of my feeling included. When I first applied I was put forward by a local adviser and when I came here I thought everyone was a bit better than me and seemed to understand everything. I said "I do not think this is me" and they said "Of course it is", so they made me feel included and now I have got a degree. I am not the most academic person, I like helping the children but it is not really me, it was a big shock to my system. I thought I could not do it and now I can actually write. You make it a bigger deal than it is. I learned to break it down and it became quite easy.

'I am a higher level teaching assistant [HLTA] but I do not work as one; I am one-to-one support for a child with mild autism aged eight years. Although he is fine in school, mum says that out of school he is hard work. In school we have so much routine it is easier for him, and at home mum has other children and so it is harder for him out of school, or he holds it all in at school and goes wild at home. So soon enough he is leaving, he is waiting for a space in a special school. His mum wants him to go there. No one in school wants him to go, as in terms of education he is doing really well, he is probably just below average. Mum is struggling at home and she feels that by putting him in a special school it is going to help her at home. I reckon she thinks it will be more laid back for him so when he goes home he will be relaxed

'This is my third year with him. After the summer holidays he did go downhill, he had had a big gap and had to get back into the routine of going to school. I must admit I was a bit like "wow", I was not expecting it as he has gone into the other years ok. He is coming back this year into Year 4 as they do not reckon he will get a place. He wants to go to a unit attached to a primary school that is pretty full. I think he will benefit if he goes to both schools. The special school has lower expectations and he is so good at Maths and literacy I feel he will get bored. He is not stupid, he will realise he can get away with doing nothing. He might enjoy it but he will fall behind. Maybe one day at the unit and the rest in mainstream.

'I have made things like visual timetables, little cards for his tenses – when, who, what, why – so I say during literacy, "ask him questions, as he forgets". The teachers try to include him as much as possible but they do make exceptions; if he wants to go off and read a book they allow it. Most teachers

I have worked with send the child off with me as his one-to-one but this year the teacher asks him "do you want to go off and work with one of the pupils?". This is really good. Teachers think I need to stay with him but he needs to become more independent and it has worked. At annual review his mum and dad said he has no friends, he is always on his own, but I said he is not. At playtime he is because he chooses to, he wants to be alone, to have his own thinking time. In class the other children do want to work with him, they love him and I think he feels included but his parents are worried because they only see a small picture. If they could come in and watch him they would see a different "him".

'I take him out to do activities like speech and language, and every time I do something I take a picture and write it down. This record of activities is given to his parents to take home so they can see what I am doing with him.

'Inclusion is about fitting the environment around the child but not to the point where they feel different. When I made him a timetable I made one for the whole class as well. It is changing things to fit them but providing for all the other children as well. I instigate things because, for example, when the teacher says we are going to work in pairs, he will not go up to someone and ask, I have to do it for him, so I instigate the social interaction for him as he does not really understand.

'All children with SEN have their own LSA. We do meet up and share ideas with each other, just with the LSAs. The teachers do not have a very big involvement if I am honest, they take a back seat. When we were doing handover to the next year the teacher looked at me and said "Ok, will you explain?" I did not like that because he is in her class, she should explain. I feel that she should be able to pick up information to be able to explain to another teacher about him. The teachers see the LSAs and think it is their job, which is quite bad. I have not had any training. I had never worked with a child with autism. I had read about it but had not met such a child. I have learned along the way and found it very interesting. As a child, the way his brain works is very interesting and he is quite fun, he makes me laugh.

'I feel he does not need a special school, we can meet his needs. He does his literacy and numeracy in the morning and then in the afternoon it is usually fun lessons like art or DT [design technology] and if he does not want to take part nine times out of ten the class teacher will let him chill out. We let him have a nap, let him have computer time early. I want him to enjoy school and if that means changing a few things there is no point him getting upset. I realise we do have to change a few things; he understands that we have to do our literacy and he is fine with that. He goes with the rules set out.'

STORIES FROM GOVERNORS/COMMUNITY MEMBERS

Ann, governor for a secondary school

'I was very happy at school, I enjoyed my schooling and I am sure that influenced why I was happy to go back into the school environment as a teacher. My sister had a horrible secondary school experience and I know that influenced her; she had too many painful and traumatic experiences, mainly with bullying – enough to make it a miserable experience. I have been happy as a teacher and I loved going to work – it was my life. As a governor I talk to kids; the more positive experiences children have with other adults the better equipped they will be to engage with other adults in the world.

'I have been a governor for two-and-a-half years at a secondary school which had undergone lots of change in status immediately before I came. When I was already working with the school a new governing body was formed and I was a Trust-appointed governor of the new governing body. The school is a Trust school and a National Challenge school because of its low GCSE results. The school was re-launched and a new governing body created with some of the old governing body and some new appointments to fit the skills audit.

'I am involved with the school in so many different ways so it helps to be clear when I have my governor's hat on. I have a lovely "Governor" gold badge. If I am going to do governor work I put my gold badge on so the staff and pupils know that I am there on the premises as a governor. We do have open access but I do need to be invited.

'I see my role as a critical friend to the head teacher and the senior management team [SMT]. I ask challenging questions about how to continue to improve outcomes for all the young people in the school. I see it as being somebody in support of the school, and who fights the school's corner. I will show my face around the school and attend parents' evenings, house assemblies and celebrations of successes. I am the chair of the achievement committee so a lot of my role is looking at data and looking at attainment. I attend the School Senate. As the chair of the achievement committee we have undertaken some student voice work and asked children what makes a successful learner in their school and fed back. I talk to heads of house, meet with subject leaders and invite them to meetings to give presentations on what is going well for them. It is critical friendship and then hard questions that you ask to keep the school on a journey of improvement. The nature of a National Challenge Trust school is that the appointed governing body is responsible to monitor the school's improvement in order to get it above the floor target and out of National Challenge. The wider role of the governor is also this very supportive pastoral part of the school community. It is an inclusive role as you are a member of the school community.

'We have a full governing body and managed to bring in community governors and parent governors. It was hard as they felt disempowered before but now we have a thriving parent council which has a voice into the governing body. My role is a chair of a subcommittee, with parent and community governors and those who know nothing about education. I mediate things because I have the understanding of an educational practitioner. I have to understand that if they are to have a voice and ask questions of the school then they need to understand the processes.

'As a member of the full governing body, one of the main drivers in school has been to increase the sense of community within and beyond the school walls. The school sits on the boundary of several districts. We try to make it a school of its community, including its feeder primary schools, its parents and its community groups. So a massive challenge was attendance as the correlation between attendance and attainment is clear. If you want to raise attendance the school has to be a community that people want to come to, not just the kids but their parents too.

'It has been a good trajectory, attendance has gone up and up – at school, at parents' evenings, assemblies, open evenings, presentations and they have adopted a house system and have award ceremonies, which is something the school did not previously do. Our emphasis is on young people taking responsibility in the school, which improves inclusion when young people are leaders in learning and behaviour and monitoring attendance. As a governor I am very responsible for the school being an inclusive place. All details are brought to school governors' meetings.

'I went into school and walked around the grounds of the school with the head [teacher] and saw fences and kids escaping out of the school in all directions, and now I see young people in learning spaces, engaging with each other. This is my definition of inclusion – it feels to me more inclusive, friendlier and a place I would want to be in. Five years ago the school was exclusively white and now it has a significant number of BME [black minority ethnic] young people and learners with EAL [English as an additional language]. It now looks a more diverse and representative school of the city.

'We have a large proportion of SEN [students], a dyslexia specialist needs unit within the school, and they have an EAL specialist teacher now. They did have a behaviour hub, which is a vile term; they do not talk about behaviour being an issue any more, they talk more about learning, emphasis on learning. They identify their most vulnerable children in each year, pick out children when they come into Year 7 who are quietly lost in the system, in the crowd, those invisible children. They provide various interventions bringing them out in a pastoral sense, in a social sense, to try to help them guised as interventions in English or Maths but [it] is really actually more about confidence, social development. They do restorative justice and have trained up lots of their pupils to manage that. They have far less exclusions. They are undersubscribed so have students who have moved from one or more other schools for not making progress. They have quite a big turnover – five to ten per cent coming in and out, many students with EAL; that is challenging. The parent council has just had a meeting of parents – Somali women, which was very eye opening to gain a wholly new perspective. Many have moved from another part of town or are travelling to a completely different area, which is hard.

'Inclusion is about everybody within a community genuinely feeling that they belong and have a right to participate in the community, and that they have a voice in the community. On the other side, to be inclusive no one must feel excluded for any reason or any sense. If you want to be inclusive, you need to look out for people who might be feeling excluded. It is like a family, so the values like loving, caring, belonging, no matter what happens you will be there.

'Inclusion in this school takes massive hard work on the ground by the head teacher relentlessly, never expecting that it could not be better day after day. You have to have everybody with a shared vision and a shared mission. When you step into a school and you inherit a staff who do not have that. You have to create the vision with you and the staff and the pupils to get any change and to be inclusive, there has to be that sense of authentic voice. We are not just paying lip service to listening to you but we are actually listening to you and responding to you and you are helping to shape the future for all of us. The SMT changed significantly, there have been new appointments.

'It is about leadership – good, strong but not hierarchical leadership. Engagement of all the stakeholders – governors, parents, any multi-agency professionals who come into contact with any aspect of the school's work. The person on Reception makes a massive difference, staff toilets make a difference, kids' toilets make a difference. I think it is about a democratic and non-hierarchical relationship where I might hear the SMT or the head teacher talking to someone mopping the floor or locking up as if they are equals. There is not a sense of hierarchy and I think that had to happen in order to help the school make progress and become more of a community and more of a functional place.

'I think the sense that it is not "them and us". Sometimes I hear [people] in institutions referring to "they" and then you have not got an inclusive community but it is not a healthy community and can quickly become dysfunctional. There is not a "they", no group exists; "they" refer to management, systems, government and then you have lack of agency in people, fragmentation. It is important what model of environment you work in: is it fragmented or is it more like a mosaic, the moving mosaic [Hargreaves 1993], where people can work independently and with others and come in and out of different groups? – this is the most powerful. In this school it is like this. Another model that is relevant to inclusion is Hart's model of participation [Hart 1992] where you have the authentic not superficial voice – one voice idea.

'I think this is my responsibility; that is why I do it. It is not a light role taking on being a governor as it is voluntary, but it could be a full time job.

It comes with an awful lot of responsibility if you take it seriously and I do. It is a crucial role if done well, with diligence and commitment. As a governing body you must keep an eye on the school progressing and being successful for every member of the community. That is why you have to listen to voices. These are communities and lifestyles which are not in common with staff and governors in school unless you appreciate the perspective that this parent might have. If a school understands the life circumstances of the pupils coming to the school it is able to work from where they are. It is a hard job, the head teacher loves it but recognises it.'

Donald, governor for a primary school

'For the past twenty years I have been working in ICT [information and communication technology] as a developer, a programmer and a systems analyst. A few years ago I trained to become a secondary school teacher in ICT and I am looking forward to completing my NQT [newly qualified teacher] year at a school. There is a primary school around the corner from me and I knew the head teacher, who lived around the corner from me. When they were looking for community governors she suggested that I apply and I've been a school governor for two years now. I was briefly the chair of governors and then the deputy chair. I am talking to you from the perspective of a secondary school teacher, a governor of a school, as well as somebody who lives in a very diverse community.

'What has really helped me understand inclusion is my teacher training and my experience as a classroom teacher. Outside my teaching experience, including my experience as a school governor, I don't think it's thought of as seriously and certainly not so intensely. At the school governors' meetings, which happen once or twice every half-term, we rarely discuss inclusion. In relation to my personal life experience, what I think influenced me in arriving at my perceptions is the fact that my father had a stroke when I was twelve years old. He was hemiplegic as a consequence so needed quite a lot of assistance getting around. So I've been exposed to helping disabled people, shall we say. It would probably be correct to call myself some sort of a carer from an early age and I understand some of the restrictions that physical disability brings.

'I am a white man, brought up in a lower middle-class background in the north of England. Where I was brought up, I don't think we had anybody from a different ethnic background other than white British though I do remember a couple of students at my schools who were from Asian backgrounds. So other than disability and the physical impairments it's not until I moved down to London that diversity became much more prominent in my life. Where I live now, and indeed at the school where I'm a governor, there are over twenty different languages spoken as first languages in the home and things have changed even more in the past 5–10 years.

'Inclusive education for me covers a lot of perspectives. It falls in line very much with equal opportunities. No matter what the child's background, ethnic origin or physical impairments they should all be included and be given equal opportunity in whatever disciplines, or whatever participation they're doing. That can obviously include cultural diversity, whether they are in care, whether English is not their first language and several other things like physical and mental disabilities and learning difficulties.

'In the governing body in the school where I am a governor there are three committees: the finance and personnel committee, the environment, communications and community committee and the standards committee, and there are seventeen governors. Most of the major decisions in the governing body are made by the finance and personnel committee along with the head [teacher], so it's a very important committee. They look at the strategic overviews and they are very, very focused on money. Monitoring the school budget and looking where the money is going, moving the money about, making sure that the governance regarding finance is correct. The standards committee should probably be much more acquainted with talking about things like inclusion and equality of opportunity within the teaching practices of the school. They are looking at the standards of the education provided within the school and whether they're being met, including the needs of the curriculum and the needs especially regarding Ofsted. So they'll probably be more involved when talking about inclusion and those sorts of topics than the other committees.

'I am on the environment, communication and community committee. On this committee we are very involved with the immediate environment of the school such as the playground facilities, the facilities within the school, the decoration of the school, the health and safety within the school, as well as the communications with parents and the local community – making sure that the letters and newsletters that are going out are correct and appropriate, reviewing the website and generally how we are reaching out to the community.

'So within a governor's perspective I don't think the word "inclusion" has ever come up at a meeting. We talk about issues around inclusion in a fairly informal way, probably because few of us have been trained in education. We are very aware that we are a governing body in a very ethnically diverse area and that we have only one black person and one Arab person on the governing body.

'The rest of us are all white middle-class with English as a first language. So we've often talked about it within that sort of remit, of trying to make sure that the governing body is more diverse and more reflective of the local community, but we have so far been quite unsuccessful. As far as inclusive education within the school is concerned, we are very much aware that there many different languages spoken as first languages within the home. We are aware of the work that the SENCOs [special educational needs coordinators] do but do not have a good understanding because governors do not get involved in the day-to-day workings of the school.

'As a governing body we will make decisions but we will be going very much from the advice of the head teacher. It is very difficult for us to overrule the head teacher if she says, for instance, that we can do without one SEN staff member. We will say are you sure that can work? It is very much the head teacher, the finance and personnel committee and the chair that will make that decision, but especially the head teacher so we're guided very much by the head teacher's advice.

'At governors' meetings we don't use the word "inclusion" often, if at all. A lot of governors are not trained in education and are not trained as educators and do not get too involved in the day-to-day running of the school. We are trying to get more involved with the daily activities of the school and the driver is our head teacher who wants us to be better educated regarding the day-to-day running of the school. There is currently an initiative for governors to be associated with individual year groups and we would be expected to attend the school at various intervals. It would be really nice going to primary school for half a day and talking to the teachers and the heads of years. In the textbook for governors, the first sentence says that we are supposed to be a critical friend, but how involved the governor needs to be in order to be critical is a grey area.

'An example of what we are working on within the environment, communications and community committee is a governors' letter/leaflet to make the governing body more visible to the local community and so it will be sent to all the parents and to the local community as a whole. It describes what the governing body does and what the individual committees do. We are thinking about the different languages we will have to translate it into and how it should look and feel so it doesn't seem too formal or too complex. We want to make sure that it reaches as many people as possible.

'An example of one of the difficulties regarding inclusion might be that when there is a travelling community coming through the area their children might attend the school for a very short period of time, and this makes it quite difficult for the teachers. The children of travellers might attend the school for just for a few days or weeks and that has happened with several children since I've been a governor.

'I think our community is quite a robust community. Even though we have all these different backgrounds and cultures we seem to get on very well as a community and there is very little tension. There is a large Turkish community, a large black community and several Eastern European communities building up and I am not aware of any serious problems or of any people feeling excluded.

'The school runs a lot of after-school clubs, including English as a second language clubs, and many of these are run by parents. We have recently started a Parents and Staff Association [PSA] which is in its infancy and I don't know how inclusive that is from the point of view of attracting people from a variety of backgrounds, but trying to make sure that the PSA reflects the local community is supposed to be part of their remit.

'There are a lot of things that make a school inclusive, for example the way the school arranges its signage and notice boards, making sure that they use images from different religious and ethnic perspectives so that students recognise their cultural experiences and backgrounds within the school.

'It also comes down to resources, how much resources you have got. In my experience as an ICT teacher I've had one student who is severely visually impaired. He couldn't see the screen and we didn't have screens big enough. That boy needed so much support that as his teacher I was spending most of the lesson with him, omitting the rest of the students for an awful lot of the lesson. Having the resources in place to allow the teacher to get on and do the job properly is very important.'

Rachel, worker for Barnardo's

'My family were from North Wales and moved to Lancashire after the war. We were all Welsh speaking and when I went to school I could not speak English at all, my oldest brother had to interpret for us. Gradually we became integrated but there was quite a lot of prejudice against us as migrants coming into the community, we got discriminatory comments. My parents were strict Methodists and embraced communities that were disadvantaged; they were quite altruistic and were both teachers. All of us were politically driven, championing the rights of minority groups. Upon reflection, what influenced my thinking were my parents' beliefs in comprehensive education as inclusive education.

'I came out of teacher training in 1969 and got a job in a mainstream primary school where I had my first experience of a child with SEN. He was in my class, had a cleft pallet and had difficulties communicating, so we worked hard to dismantle other people's perceptions of him. I saw my role to promote positive images and ensure that he was involved and included, not segregated, with activities that enabled him to communicate and interact with others in the class.

'I then got a job in a special school as I wanted to find out, what do they do? What is special education? It was a school for children with behavioural issues, a new school with a great committed staff of teachers. Children explored the curriculum through doing things rather than a strict task-based range of activities, they had external experiences out of school so they were not so isolated. We had good support from educational psychology who helped the teachers to create a stimulating learning environment. The speech therapist worked in the class with the children. The children had experience of community projects – helping with a litter campaign in the shopping precinct, which impacted on people's attitudes towards the children and the school. The children were out in the community, in the environment rather than segregated in the special school.

'In the next school for learners with moderate learning difficulties we took the thematic experiential approach as it was just as relevant for these children. We did a lot of work to develop curriculum that was experientially based across the age range and this was successful. Then I moved to Cornwall and had my children. Cornwall did not have special schools so Statemented children were in the mainstream schools. That made me question that if these children can be integrated, why not for all the others, what is different?

'In the next special school we planned a cycle of life skills projects, out in the community for children, developing core skills for the children and involving the families. Looking outwards rather than inwards and incorporating what the community could contribute as well. At this time the children's right to have access to the national curriculum that was relevant to them came about, and provided them with skills; this was a great step towards inclusive education. I worked with a teacher who had a class of learners with profound and multiple learning difficulties who created a multi-sensory structure for them and knew what the children responded to.

'My next post was in another special school as a manager. I was to oversee the merger of children from the most disadvantaged backgrounds with learning disabilities and emotional issues with twenty children from a school for learners with complex physical disabilities. People were very concerned about putting the different groups together, with the greatest resistance from staff at the physical disability school. We organised a lot of disability equality work with disabled children talking to the other children about their access issues and needs. They talked together before the amalgamation about sharing the playground to ensure no one was in danger and eventually they became friends. We noted that there was a softening of behaviours from quite aggressive children who would sit calmly with the disabled children. There was mutual benefit of being together. It also toughened up the disabled children too.

'Gradually the lessons were more and more integrated until they did not have separate lessons at all. I thought, if this can work here with potentially challenging youngsters, why can it not work in mainstream schools? The staff attitudes were the most difficult; I believe that if you want it to work and you have the right attitude, it can work. The school would never invite parents into school, no carol concerts or harvest festivals; to change that culture was really hard as I believe that all children had an entitlement to cultural experiences. We tried to influence local community attitudes towards children in the school. It was particularly challenging with the difficult behaviour of the children, and children on the Child Protection Register where communities whose management of their children is very different and alien to our expectations in school. Without criticising them or saying "yours is a deficit model and ours isn't", you need to come to a context where you can safely explore some of the issues.

'We had discos after school and a brilliant cook who would do the chips and get beer in. We would have a massive turnout of parents and grandparents after the disco when they came to pick their kids up. They could sit for an hour and have a bag of chips, a beer and a chat and we could talk with them. It is not about parents' evenings, it is about opening up your doors. The role of the teacher is to create that environment of respect for learners and for families.

'I retired from teaching and took up a role with Barnardo's to develop the inclusion of pupils into further education based on the Tomlinson Report [Tomlinson 1996]. Children were coming through mainstream comprehensive schools and had aspirations to go on to FE [further education] with their peers, so the challenge was to create an inclusive framework in the FE college. It was a three-year project attempting to implement the community-based experiential methodology onto an FE provision.

'My job was to develop the institution so that the students could participate at curriculum level, social level and academic level. We looked at the physical environment, did an audit, did an audit of the curriculum, of training needs for the staff, looked at the menu of entitlement for tutorial work, how it supported students; many strategies to understand what inclusion meant for everyone. Every year they had an equalities week to look at all discrimination. We tried to build on this to explore how do we learn from each other, how do we use the curriculum to create social inclusion, how do we use the tutorial system to safely talk about discrimination, what do they not understand about disability? How can we get positive role models of lecturers who have a disability? My colleague was a blind person and we worked together, a disabled trainer came in too, which became a powerful message to be working alongside disabled tutors as professionals and tutors. This was a big key message for students experiencing discrimination.

'The curriculum project started with the school of engineering to design a piece of equipment for a disabled person. They asked Barnardo's to come and talk about disability so I said "You need a disabled person". So from that starting point we recruited disabled children and adults in the community to work with the students. They realised that they could communicate with disabled people and that they had the same opinions and aspirations. The disabled people wanted a sex life, to get married, to socialise, they wanted a nice home environment to help them to access things and go out with their mates. This inclusion process was about positive images of normality. Two young men went into a disabled person's home to design a seat for her bath. They sat down and talked to her, lay on the floor looking at her feet and talking to her with such empathy and thoughtfulness. Those two people would go out a new generation of engineers with no barriers to participating with disabled persons. Those were the kind of things that created an inclusive environment in the college.

'This was a three-year piece of work which developed from engineering into fashion into literature and the writing of stories and poetry. We completed audits of the physical building, and the dining area became more accessible so students could participate at lunchtime together. Over three years it became a much more inclusive organisation but the curriculum was the root of the change. Students went to a disabled couple's wedding and designed their clothes for the wedding. They became their friends and not "disabled people" any longer. It has been disabled colleagues who really challenged me in my work – we worked together and began to trust each other to be able to develop provision.

'Barnardo's worked with the local shops and businesses, the Chamber of Commerce, to get them on board welcoming disabled people and students into the work community from the college. Similar to the community-based experiential methodology of the primary curriculum, we were going into the community to find experiences for FE learners which the community could participate in together. It is about the context in which learning takes place. Each year we had an exhibition of exclusive technology so that others could see what ICT equipment, what software for computers was there for them, which was really inclusive. It deepened the partnership with the Chamber of Commerce as it enabled potential employers to see the technology that existed to support disabled people into employment.

'Barnardo's was also commissioned to consult with children in care following a series of reports from government about the under-achievement of looked-after children. We did a consultation with eleven- to fourteen-year-olds, and what emerged was that it was not about resources but about people's attitudes towards them. I listened to the looked-after children talking about the way they were bullied in school, the way teachers' perceptions were very negative, the lack of dialogue with their foster carers, the lack of training of foster carers, very similar to the experiences of disabled children.

'A further consultation with disabled young people called Have Your Say identified people's perceptions of them as the greatest barrier. One young man explained about a woman at a careers event who looked at him as he said "I want to go into IT" and she said "You want to learn to make a cup of tea?" and he said "No, I do not want to go to college to learn how to make a cup of tea, I want to go to college to learn IT". He explained that "she looked at my wheelchair and she did not hear me at all".

'Parent Partnership commissioned Barnardo's to consult with children in mainstream schools who had additional funding to access support needs. The authority wanted to know if the money was used effectively from the child's perspective. All the children were in mainstream schools. We went to secondary schools and primary schools and what emerged from those children with learning difficulties and physical impairments was about the culture of the school and the attitudes of staff. It was so clear that children could articulate what their needs were in the outstanding school working with learners with difficult behaviours. One girl said "I get the fidgets and I find it really hard so I go down to the sunshine room, it is ok to go there.

I get myself together and then I go back". Another boy said "I know how it is, when I get bad I cannot understand what they are saying, so I go out. I go to the library and the librarian says sit down and when you are ready you can go back". It was not "What are you doing? Why are you out of class?", it was about how each child learns to manage their own behaviour. These young-sters were identifying staff attitudes, how they were treated as a positive contribution to their inclusion in mainstream school.

'The Index for Inclusion [Booth and Ainscow 2011] and the UNICEF Rights-Respecting Schools [Awards] are useful frameworks and schools that use these approaches have noticed a significant change in prejudiced type behaviour and it has also influenced the way staff speak to each other and behave towards children. It is about high standards of human interactions. The school where the children understood their own needs led to enhanced respect.

'An external organisation like Barnardo's can be a critical friend, an external body working outside the school in the community, and be more creative to support curriculum development by encouraging partner commu-nity organisations to engage with schools and explore learning together. I was the catalyst to do that. I had credibility because I had been a teacher, not just a Barnardo's worker; you had to prove yourself as a practitioner to be accepted. You have to demonstrate that you can engage with disabled chil-dren, with learners with difficulties and mainstream learners. I walked into a large group of motor vehicle engineers in the classroom all sitting there with their feet on the tables. I said could you get your feet off the table please, they all did. They engaged with my colleague, who was blind and leading the lecture, and I was supporting and contributing. We talked about bullying and hit them quite hard; they listened well. We had a good discussion.

'Inclusion is based around the rights and respecting agenda. It is not just what happens in the school, it is about inclusion of parents, inclusion of extended families and how they are part of the school and respected. School is not the only vehicle through which children and young people learn. They come into school with experiences that can inform the school. A parent who was a builder, we went out to visit his building site with the class, which was a very good experience for everyone but particularly for the child, who felt so proud. It is about respect for the learner within the school and within the local community. It is about practising the rights and respect consistently. If all the public services for children, young people and their families work together then it can become a strong, inclusive school community to protect children and support their learning, a collective approach.

'A community school is a socially inclusive school which has a two-way process of communication between the school and community.'

STORIES FROM EDUCATIONAL PSYCHOLOGISTS

Joyce, early years educational psychologist

'I am an early years senior educational psychologist. I work for the County Council. I have been a practising psychologist for four years and I am in my thirties. I feel very strongly about inclusion. I understand it in terms of physical and social inclusion. With social inclusion we consider the environment where children feel part of a group and are able to make relationships, be a productive member of a particular group, whether they feel included within that. Sometimes this is through physical inclusion, sometimes this is, as in any social group, where one feels included. I feel that inclusion can be a reflective state which is not always measurable but can be a very personal feeling to the individual.

'What shaped my views about inclusion is working closely and developing relationships with the family, gaining an insight into what life is like for them as parents or carers of children with complex needs.

'When discussing inclusion, it is important that everybody has an understanding of what inclusion is and what it means to them because we can all talk about how a child becomes included within an educational provision but often individuals have different perceptions of what that is. And, as part of any process really, [to ensure] that we have that common understanding, that common language, because inclusion can mean different things to different people and at different stages of a child's life. The different aspects of the child: are they included physically, socially, emotionally and educationally? Have we asked them what would help them be part, become included? A big part of our role is to find out what this child likes, what the child thinks, what would help them.

'With inclusion as an early years educational psychologist, children often don't have the voice. And it is quite often the case with the children I work with, who, if they come to me at such a young age, usually have very complex needs and require quite complex provision. So my role there is to, really, initially get to know the family and to help them deal with let's say diagnosis, or deal with the knowledge that their child will need extra support in some way. What does it mean to cover complex needs, what does it mean for them, and with the inclusion part of it quite often when education is brought up, then it will be about what can you hope for your child, what sort of education, what education is appropriate? These are questions that parents come to me and ask me and together – through, let's say using an early support approach, which is what we use, where it is very much about working in partnership with the family – coming up [with] what . . . we feel is the best for the child. And sometimes it is through assessments, through just talking with the parents, finding out about what they feel the child's education should be like.

'The assessments that I will carry out would most generally cover all areas of development so they would look at the child's fine motor skills, their gross motor coordination; [they] would also focus on self-help and independence skills, as well as play, early learning skills and language.

'We would make sure that they have IEPs [individual education plans] written that are relevant to that child, that are reflected in the Statement, in the long-term objectives, that the targets are broken down at the level where children can achieve, therefore helping facilitate inclusion, helping them achieve along with their peers to their level of ability.

'So you would have a very broad assessment and with that you identify what is their skill base, what are their abilities, what are their functional abilities, and then you see what is the next step.

'As an EdPsych [Educational Psychology] service, the children are at the centre. We also ensure that policies and practices are in the early support work, using the Common Assessment Framework [CAF], working in partnerships with other professionals, ensuring that children do not slip through the net. When it is done well and it has worked, the team around the child can be very productive and lead to far more immediate services.

'As an educational psychologist, certainly the social part of inclusion is very important because we deal with the emotions of the children, their social interaction, their skills, very much at an interaction level, as well as considering their learning. Are they able to be included and achieve alongside their peers? As educational psychologists, we help equip teachers to be able to include the children within the school and provide that supportive role to both the adults as well as to the children themselves.

'I would like to draw on a secondary school pupil as an example, in terms of a child, a young lady [who] presented with quite significant social and emotional needs. She was in a secondary school yet she was quite fearful to come to school, therefore it made inclusion very difficult for her. She did not feel part of the school, she did not want to go to her mainstream secondary school, and so she had quite significant phobias . . . and they were all linked to degenerative eye difficulties that she had, or that was what we established through our conversations, that that was the start of it, through finding out what she is like, what is troubling her, asking those questions that have perhaps not been asked of her before. I find that quite common, in terms of . . . a lot of young people say to me "nobody has asked me about this before".

'In my experience, the quality of services aimed at inclusion vary across authorities and even within the same authority. I believe to an extent its success depends on how willing professionals are to help the family; that is, individual professionals and when they are working together.'

Carol, tutor for training of educational psychologists

'When I was a university student I got some holiday work in a psychiatric hospital in Ireland, for two summers; they allocated me to work on their children's unit. It was a pretty appalling set-up with the most diverse range of kids in it. Children with profound and multiple difficulties and children I would now recognise as being on the autistic spectrum, to those who were actually young offenders. All lobbed in together. I think that experience really sparked my interest in children.

'I trained as a teacher of children deemed to be "educationally subnormal" and worked in a special school for several years before I wanted a change and was starting to question why some of the children ended up in the special school. I thought maybe I need to understand this more and go to the other side and see what happens there. I met up with a researcher who was exploring how learners who were gifted and talented might be provided for in mainstream schools, and had the opportunity for to work half in a research capacity with him and the other half as a peripatetic supply teacher confined to the special schools in the borough.

'I had a roving brief for all the special schools. I ended up teaching in all of them throughout the year, which was very interesting. The research work involved going into loads of primary schools because my brief was to work with the teachers to get them to identify from their classes a range of individuals, with input and awareness raising, that they thought might be gifted and talented. I, under the guidance of the psychologist, would do some baseline cognitive assessments with them. This early experience of so many different schools within a single borough led me to question the placement of learners in special or mainstream contexts. I had great fun taking all these different classes in all these different schools and it became clear to me that actually where children end up, how they get designated and viewed, is pretty arbitrary and more to do with the settings they are in despite their individual differences and individual needs.

'Then educational psychology kind of crystallised in my mind and I decided to go and train. I was lucky to do my training at the university where Sheila Wolfendale was the new course director, who had very inclusive ideas and believed in working with parents and communities, which impacted on me.

'I did my final dissertation about two speech and language units attached to mainstream schools; the children never spent more than fifty per cent of their time in the unit and so were at least fifty per cent in the mainstream. They had speech therapists. The study was around the teachers' perceptions in the mainstream school and their knowledge base. On my EP [educational psychologist] training programme I worked as a portage worker with a family, which gave me insight into the needs of a family in the early years of a child.

'Change was starting to happen at that time; the special school I had worked in was originally a school for learners with moderate learning difficulties [MLD], [and] colleagues began thinking about change starting from the ground up. They pushed to be allowed to go out and spend some of their time supporting children in mainstream schools instead of having them always come into the special school. It was quite dramatic in that special school, but it split the staff in half as to whether they thought it was a good idea.

'The role of the educational psychologist is a very hard space to make changes from, unless there are key people already embedded in that setting or community whose attitudes and motivation to change are there already. Once you have that kernel there are lots of things you can do to help support and build. Unless you can find that kernel somewhere it is very difficult to bring about change.

'You are expected to be able to work directly with children, support staff, teachers and you have the opportunity to work with senior management of schools. You are expected to be good at working with parents, especially where there are issues or conflict with the education system. You are also required to be involved in and advising the local authority in various policy and strategies, it is in the statutory role. We are frequently involved on the training side as well as working with parents. You also have to understand about child development and processes of attachment. So you could take any bit of that and find other professionals that were equally experienced, but as a whole package together there are not many people who span the whole of it.

'I went to a local education officer and presented a case about a small group of children. I explained that he would have the families pushing for financial support to enable their children to go to independent school. I knew a secondary school who would be willing and committed to support these youngsters if a proper package could be put together to enable them to do it. I explained that even from the financial side it would be worthwhile for the authority. In those days education officers could say "Ok, let's do it". I spent a lot of time in my role with parents, actually separately with the parents and separately with the school to prepare them for the angst that would come through this change process. The secondary school ended up being resourced through the local authority, not just for the specific group of children but to take six or eight places for children with high-level needs and use that support flexibly. It was really interesting to work with the school and see how they developed. We also looked at effective use of learning support assistants (LSAs), not just Velcro LSAs, and did a lot of work supporting the parents.

'The new academy school structures have been able to set their own admissions policy, so it is far more difficult for any intervention at an authority-wide level to have any impact on this. On the broader political level, this challenge does not seem to be impinging on anyone's conscious-ness. There is no good having committed people if they are not at a level in the organization or system to be able to influence change.

'In a number of areas, the multi-agency panels are still having discussions between social care and the medical world about whether it is a good idea to keep a child included in the mainstream school. They still are saying "Why not go into a special school?" This is the usual way unless you have a depth of understanding about the education process or the multi-agency teams listen to the educationalist. There has not been that work done to get everybody talking together, so we have gone several steps backwards. We continue to have many people suggesting that these children could be better off in a special school. They do not have enough understanding of schools and the education system to be thinking "actually, if this school was doing things differently these issues would not be arising".

'If you want people to come together to do something, it is not the people, not the where and the when, but it is the piece of work. If you can identify pieces of work that everyone can buy into and all see themselves as being able to contribute, then allowing them to do those pieces of work will actually enable the best framework to emerge to support them in working together. You do not start with the framework, you start with the pieces of work and the relevant people to contribute to it.

'As an educational psychologist you have a better idea of all the different parts that are required to join together to make an inclusive school community. An educational psychologist can act like a catalyst if the opportunities are there and are spotted, you can make the connections. More dialogue with schools would enable the educational psychologist to get through to the ones that really need attention. When the educational psychology team was allocated time in schools then parents were able to see them in the school. If social care could have a stronger link with school it could be beneficial. I cannot understand why the whole area of social care is not more entwined into the education system as most of the indicators and concerns emerge through the school. The schools do notice but no one [else] takes any notice so this is the weak link.

'Educational psychologists no longer require Qualified Teacher Status (QTS) before they qualify, only experience in settings with children, young people and families. So learning mentors, social care workers and speech and language therapists are coming forward to qualify as educational psychologists. They are given the space and time in training to sit together and talk about their roles and differences, which is very important. The impact of this on inclusive education could potentially be very positive.'

Janet, early years educational psychologist

'What shaped a lot of my thinking is that my father was a fundamental Baptist minister, hell and fire and brimstone and very prejudiced, "do as I say not as I do". My father was half Native American and my mother was a southern girl brought up on a plantation, a strong person. I left home and went to fundamental bible college to train for the mission field as my family had expected. This did not work out so eventually I got into teachers' college. I was disowned by my father when I was in teachers' college because I changed my religion. I had been excluded from my family and was the black sheep for a long time, which is what made me and I bring that into my job. I had an inward calling and had to shift my thinking from missionary work to work with children with problems and learning difficulties.

'I started working at a state institution in the USA, a diagnostic clinic for autistic spectrum disordered [ASD] children and learning difficulties; we called it "mental retardation" in those days. I was an assistant and learned a lot about treatment, about families and about attitudes. There were no options about inclusion, it was all about exclusion. For most of the kids it was about being assessed and then leaving their home to go into institutions as there were no special facilities for such children. I witnessed how parents were torn, watching their breakdowns as they sent their children off, scared children as their parents walked away leaving them in cribs alone and scared. This was shaping me. I opened up the first class for children with specific learning difficulties in the US; we used much patterning and ocular exercises, processing deficit activities. This was the first class within primary mainstream school, the first taste of inclusion, self-contained within a mainstream school.

'I did my Master's in elementary education with an emphasis in special education. Then I opened up the first resource room for junior high students, all boys, then opened the same thing but in secondary school. I was asked to teach evening and summer school courses for the university and the private college.

'I got a job as a self-contained specific learning difficulties teacher in a mainstream school and began to open specific classes. The principal had strong views on inclusive education. I had also strong feelings from my background in a separatist family and not liking it much. I worked in the UK for three years in a middle school and in special education and then returned to the US where I became a diagnostician, in a clinic for two years. We would interview the kids failing in schools, and the teachers. They came to us for six weeks and we convinced the schools to take them back based on our plans and actions. There were eight of us in the diagnostic unit, four were teachers of learners with learning difficulties and four teachers of learners with emotional and behavioural difficulties. I learned a lot about the impact of behaviour on learning but we struggled to get the kids back into schools and teachers accepting them. They often had to change schools as the teachers would not accept them. It was to be a revolving door situation but the attitudes were horrific.

'During my doctorate programme I was functioning as a school psychologist in early years. In the USA they were looking at different types of multi-agency working arrangements, trans-disciplinary work. People came and did training about this trans-disciplinary working in early years, looking at dynamic play-based assessment rather than formal assessments. In the same school district in the early 1990s I worked on a new initiative with social workers and education, to support whole families with disabilities. I had gone through the history of integration, several years of doing formal assessments on children through to the change of ideology into trans-disciplinary work, meeting the needs of the whole child in the context of the family.

'My doctorate supervisor was a strong inclusionist, he really questioned special schools and special classes and why differentiation could not go on. At that time I was put in a position where recommendations and programmes were only in special provisions. I wrestled with that, a soul-searching dilemma, was it right or wrong positioning? He talked me through this to decide how as an EP [educational psychologist] you do the best for the child; it may not always be what you think is most appropriate, but you have to work through that.

'I had had those experiences of prejudice and exclusion earlier in life so I felt very strongly about inclusion and had a good understanding of the emotional impact that exclusion can have on children and adults. On my training programme there were people with very different views about inclusion so we had much discussion about it. The professors were rather behaviourist but I learned that everything had to be argued about. We had much discussion, nothing was given – how do you know it works? All our papers had to be evidence-based. That background where everything was questioned was so eye-opening, enabling us to look at others' perspectives.

'My work as an EP has changed from the "expert model" of approaching children and their problems to exploring the whole child, a non-expert model, and working together to meet the needs of the child within the context of the family that is the "multi-agency approach".

'I feel very strongly about inclusion but feel that for some children, maybe inclusion is not the best place for them. It all depends on the individual setting. The setting determines whether the child's needs can be met, it may not always be possible. My responsibility as an EP is to support schools in making the accommodation and the curriculum and social and emotional aspects fully differentiated for the child.

'I am a reformer; I have turned around a lot of things in the early years inclusion service and portage service. It is strategic, moving the practices on and bringing people on with me because I have lived those experiences in the USA. I have a clear idea, but it takes a while to get there.'

STORIES FROM SOCIAL WORKERS

Martin, social worker without a case load based in an educational setting

'I was a normal statutory social worker qualified to work with adults and children but I chose childcare and have been doing it for six years. When I first started sitting in on Common Assessment Framework [CAF] panels I got a sight of multi-agency working or inclusion. I see these two as very similar. For me as a social worker I was able to make links with other professionals in one place through the fortnightly CAF panels. I got to meet professionals from other agencies on a regular basis that I had not been able to do before.

'Usually, in your role as a social worker you come into contact with other professionals, but not in such a regular way so you can start to build up a relationship with other agencies through the CAF process. That was important for me – I saw how I could make links, to get to know each other, to share information about cases and about our professional knowledge. It was really helpful for my development as a social worker. I could see how inclusion into a mainstream school worked for the child and family as well, having all the agencies around in one place, seeing each other, sharing information, all understanding how we can support and help.

'My role is entitled an "Early Intervention Social Care Worker" and is a relatively new post. It came about because the head of a local secondary school had a frank conversation with Social Care about miscommunications and misunderstandings that were occurring between them. They wanted to create a post that would help to improve the situation. They suggested a Social Care professional to sit between the two agencies, but not to have a case load, so not to have to spend time with children, young people and families. The Extended Schools Partnership at the time agreed that some capacity building needed to be done. It was not about taking cases away from schools, it was about learning, breaking down misunderstandings, information sharing between the two agencies – schools and social care in this locality. It did not really involve Health Services, just Social Care. The post was born because Social Care put some money in, but most of the money came from the Extended School Partnership, based in the education sector. This partnership has disbanded now but the role was so successful that it has been continued at least for another year.

'My role focuses on making the connections and the relationships that the teachers and social workers in statutory provision do not have time to do. It is about finding out where the best relationship links are and who to include. Sometimes you do not need to include a lot of people as too many people can be overkill. I will look at the situation and say "Ok, the head teacher is really busy today but the deputy has got more time and he is really good, so talk to the deputy".

'What this post has shown me is that if you are willing to think a little bit out of the ordinary you can make things work. I support fifteen schools; at the start I spent a day in every school so that I could be oriented and see how differently each school operates. I sat in the classes, talked to staff and had lunch with the kids – them getting to know me and me getting to know them. I then had a focused staff meeting to share my role with the staff, I prepared a handout outlining my role and they could ask questions or give me a call. I came to understand what the school day looked like rather than simply having someone tell me. I found that so much is packed into a school day and I found out why teachers were not able to call anyone until the end of the day, when the children go home.

'The concept of inclusion, my first and remaining concept, is that I can do my job better when I am working with people. My team background is working in social work teams. So I have my social work team, my colleagues and my manager, and then we have the building team, those who work in this building. We have got an asylum seekers team, adult support, catering staff and reception. I feel that if I get to know as many people as possible they will all help me to do my job. A lot is me: the way I think, bit of personal, bit of cultural. A lot has come from learning. I had a good team manager driving it into you to talk with others – she emphasised the value of building relationships. She said "even when things are going ok, keep in touch with the professionals involved with all the children you are allocated".

'So inclusion is about building good working relationships that enable you to work better for the children who are at the centre of our job. It is the children we are trying to protect, so together we will be able to provide a better service.

'I have my own information-sharing protocol as I mediate between people, so I give out telephone numbers and names, but I have not had my wrists slapped yet and there has been no bloodshed. I always check up and ask, but I have not had a difficulty when it comes to dealing with the welfare and well-being of children. We are all working for the child. I see the professional I am sharing information with is connected with that child and if they were not connected with the child I would not be sharing the information. Maybe if information is behaviour-related, it gives teachers a useful background to the behaviour. Sometimes they will not have a clue why the child is behaving like this and then both the child and the staff are at risk. I will make a professional judgement and if the child is in their school and I decide it is relevant, I share the information. I could look at it and withhold it but if I think the information will help them to manage or support the child in their school, then I share the information. This is important to enable inclusive education for all children and young people.

'Families will say "I do not want Social Services knocking on my door". It is usually us they do not want. Schools usually have the better relationships with their families and so they can support the social worker into the families. With Social Care tapping into the school correctly they can gain a lot of information about the child and about the family just by having the right relationships with the school. It is about building good professional relationships to help you as a social worker to do your job better

'You have to think differently; school is your best friend if you are a social worker. If you have a good relationship, the information will flow backwards and forwards between the two agencies. You have to build trust and it takes time.

'The strategy I use is to practise with a double mindset. You have your mindset as a teacher or a social worker from your background and training, but you also have the opposite social work/teacher in your mind at the same time; maybe this is a new skill, a kind of empathy. If you are going to be a multi-agency worker, you will need to understand many others and you will need to "bear them in mind". We need to share the risk, share the concern and share the information. Each professional should share what we can do in our capacity as a social worker, and the health visitor will share what they can do in their capacity as a health visitor. We match the information together. The more agencies we include and share together, the bigger the safety net we provide for children, young people and families, but one agency cannot do it all: we have to work together.

'We are trying to share practices. I will share with schools how a social worker works, I have a presentation, The Role of the Social Worker, that I give to schools. Schools did not understand how social workers worked and social workers did not understand how schools worked and this was creating massive communication problems and understanding problems. We have shared information. I explain that social workers [each] have an average of thirty cases; some of those cases are looked-after children and some of the cases are child protection, so I give some scenarios

'We do this crossing-over of information. If the social workers are getting frustrated they ask me to find out what is going on in that school. I used to do a lot of mediation but now I often say why do you not just talk to the head [teacher] – his number is x, just ring him on Tuesday afternoon because I know he is free. I am pushing people together and stepping out. I will tell the head that he is going to get a call and he will say lovely, so I make sure things happen.

'I can divert concerns from becoming a Social Care referral, so everyone benefits. There were too many calls going to Social Care which they cannot deal with, and this does not happen anymore. The staff in schools will always have grey-area questions and I am able to take all those questions. I know there is no such thing as a stupid question.

'I have done it with Housing as well. One of the high schools was getting a high rate of parents saying they were going to throw their kids out. The teachers were at their wits' end, this is like a Housing situation so what can we do about this? I had a contact in Housing so I got in touch with him and said "look, this situation is developing in school, can you talk to them?". He said "Yes, I would love to. I have been trying to get into school for ages". So I gave him the number and suggested a time to call and just talk to Jacky so they could sort it out. Next thing I knew they had organised a meeting. So it is just pushing people together instead of pushing people apart because the information is wrong. A couple of sentences, couple of emails and phone call, talk to each other, have a meeting, half an hour will not take long really. I have got workers from the local Housing department talking to the teachers in school through really simple interventions. Now highly complex social concerns for young people can be explored to ease the pressure on young people and enable them to focus on their learning.

'When I approach the parents, I always say I am working for the school. I am able to sort things out quickly because I do not have other cases. I am able to [devote] concentrated, dedicated time to that situation, to that parent, and the results you get are good because you have the time to do it. You can find out how young people are doing, catch up and talk, you see them in school, in the street. I see them more than their social worker would and that is the truth. I have the freedom to move around the schools as well. I am also able to balance my time as some parents you need to concentrate on more than others, so it works both ways.'

Sarah, social worker in a disabled children's team

'I did the CQSW [Certificate of Qualification in Social Work] in 1979, and because I was funded through the Home Office, once I qualified I became a probation officer and stayed with probation service for over twenty years apart from having children. Then I worked for a charity called Prison, Me? No Way!, which involved prison officers going into schools and youth groups and talking with young people about what being in prison really was like, what sort of people went there, what treatment they got, and what a cell was like. I did that for eighteen months before the project closed down in this area because the money stopped. I started with the disabled children's team as I did not want to work in child protection. I work with the short-break team which is working only with disabled children and their families. I also do assessments on people who want to become short-break carers or family-link carers for disabled children. I take the application to a panel that looks at the application and approves them and then you link the carer to the disabled child and their family.

'This job requires a children's social worker as you are coordinating services for the child and you are acting as an advocate for the child. You are not their parent but you say what you think might be best for the child. You also attend reviews with the school staff to put the child's views forward. Sometimes people do underestimate the resilience of kids, what they can actually cope with – moving house, divorce, changing situation, people dying; they cope well, often better than adults

'It depends upon the level of the disability as to whether inclusion in education and in play is a good idea. I think if it is suitable and works best for the child then yes, it should be encouraged and promoted. You look at the child, their abilities, their needs and their level and their ability to cope

'I think living in a small village can be more inclusive than living in a city because people know you and everybody is more likely to accept that you have a disability, can understand and relate to you.

'I went to see a little boy, six years old, in mainstream school. He has cerebral palsy and has very little movement in his arms, already in a wheelchair sitting quite hunched. His brain is very fast, so as long as the school is accessible to a disabled child he should be fine. He should go right through primary and secondary provision and use modern technology to enable him to be something, to enable him to go out into the world. However, you can already see that life will be ten times harder for him than any other child, he will have to prove himself to [people]. [They] will see the disability first and the child second, even though we are trying to educate people to see the child first and then the disability. It would be awful sending him to a special school as intellectually he is miles ahead of all the other children. He likes a chat, this little lad; he cannot run around, but with support and encouragement I think he will keep up.

'It is a big step up for any child, going to senior school, but for a child using a wheelchair it is very hard. The physicality of senior schools, they are big compared to the little primary school and have all the different teachers. One teacher in the primary school, many in secondary with different approaches to how they work with the children, that is hard. Also socially, everyone in the junior school knew you, they loved you, they accepted you in the wheelchair and they threw the ball to you in the playground. Suddenly you are going into this enormous school with hundreds of children who look at you and ask "What is wrong with you?" That must be very hard for a child. I am thinking how much preparation the primary school must give to that child for that transition to work.

'The parents of autistic children often feel that inclusion was disabling the child rather than empowering them as they are so different. The lack of education and understanding demonstrated by teachers in mainstream schools with regards to autism, and its various degrees on the spectrum, were putting these children at a major disadvantage. Many parents recount having their child in mainstream, not being happy, withdrawing them, putting them in a special school which dealt purely with autistic children and their children flourishing because they did not feel odd, they did not feel different or that people were laughing at them or undermining them. The staff understood the children because they had experience working with autistic children. The routines were so much more defined and clear to an autistic child so they were not thrown into panic attacks all the time. The level of support was higher in the special schools because it was provided in a different way. In mainstream, school children would have a one-to-one LSA with them, which again makes you stand out from the others, and children ask "What is wrong with you?" If you have an adult sitting next to you all the time you can feel isolated or over-dependent on them.

'The life of a disabled child can be very narrow; it does not grow but it stays very narrow. It is not just within school, it is the whole social network, and it is life. The role of the social worker is to push them to meet more people. Through respite care the children may have different types of experience from those their parents can provide. Sometimes respite carers might take a disabled child to the balloon fair or down to the sea or to the zoo. The carers have some financial support and so can give children a wider range of experiences. It is good when they go for short breaks as they do sleep in a different bedroom and do other things and eat different foods and do different activities, and if there are other children in the family of the short break carer, then they make new friends.

'We are developing a project here for bridging workers, whose role would be to offer advice for families to make links into the community. They go out to the family of the disabled child, meet them and ask about what social activities the child might wish to do, e.g. if he wants to join the Scouts or go swimming. The bridging worker then links the services appropriate to the child's needs and wishes and either the parent or the short break carer will take them along to the events. It is hoped that they will then start accessing events in the community. It is about inclusive play with non-disabled facilities; these are growing now.'

Alex, qualified social worker and teacher based in a residential special school

'On reflection, my own secondary school education had an impact – I was classified as a slow learner in secondary school, later in life to be recognised as dyslexic, but in school I was criticised for not paying attention and not being able to do my work in the way other people did it. That led to an outcome of challenging behaviour where I was in trouble quite a lot in school. The second thing was when the PE teacher organised a 24-hour sponsored badminton session and he sexually abused one of my friends during the night. He gave everybody cider and we were only fourteen years old. These incidents led to my commitment to safeguarding children socially and educationally.

'I left school and went on to be an engineer and had a blinkered perception of social values because I worked in a ninety-five per cent male workforce, and in terms of equality and diversity there was a rather sexist humour that went on. After several years of night school to gain a degree I was made redundant and decided to go and train as a teacher of design and technology [DT]. I had been working in a residential special school during my training and once I qualified as a teacher the same school gave me a job as a DT teacher, doing a bit of health and safety as well. I worked with the kids during the day and during the evening and eventually decided to go and work in the care side. I really enjoyed this and found that I was actually quite good at it; other staff would ring me up if they had problems with the young people. I decided to train as a social worker and learned how to empower service users to take the maximum control over their lives and that every young person or adult needs to feel valued and celebrated and encouraged to enhance their independence skills.

'I am now the quality assurance officer at school. I ensure policies are upheld and we comply with current legislation in terms of health, education and care for children and vulnerable adults. I have a breadth of thinking because of my dual qualification – qualified teacher and qualified social worker. I use bits of my social work training and bits of my education training; both aspects are required to work with challenging young people. The emphasis in education is on progress and learning, so the evaluation schedule from Ofsted can be very challenging. As a social care worker, education appears as an oppressive system: kids are forced to go to school. The way they are disciplined and the behaviour expectations are different from a social worker's view.

'A social worker would be asking "are this person's basic human needs being met, of food, warmth, love, supportive family, somewhere to sleep at night?" The role is about meeting their life needs as social workers. Teachers argue that they impact on learning of life skills through education and if they do not get the skills to be able to achieve economic well-being then the cycle of deprivation will perpetuate. So there is a good argument for both approaches. Inclusion is the key for me, but both sets of frameworks – education and social care – need to be a bit more malleable and less rigid than they are now, to make it work for all children and young people.

'In my role as a part-time Ofsted inspector I have come across several new school communities with overall funding for mainstream primary, mainstream secondary and special school on the same site, the same community but with different provision. Learners from the special school go and attend lessons in the mainstream setting and learners from the mainstream come and get additional support in the special school. This is not the same as everyone being in the same class and being able to access things but it is a good model of inclusion. Everybody is going to the same place and everybody is mixing together some of the time. Also, in terms of understanding diversity, learners are being mixed and educated together at the same time; it is better than being separate.

'The dream would be someone designing an environment and educational practices that are accessible to a wide range of individuals within the same setting. That will not happen with class sizes of thirty with one teacher. It would need classes of five to ten with some additional support and take a different style of education; training of teachers would need to be different, but it could be inclusive.

'I have come across my social work colleagues providing support for those young people who were looked after, as this is the only input our current legislative framework allows for social workers to have in a school setting. Social workers can also work in schools within areas of deprivation which also recognises some anti-social behaviour. In mainstream schools where there are behaviour problems, the social worker can act as a kind of inclusion officer, a behaviour management type role – pastoral, getting them into class, interface with parents, home visits, lateness, attendance, the bits the senior management did not want to do. This could be an interesting role to develop in support of inclusion.

'I can see that inclusion is important, but as a social worker I would need to reflect on whether that is what those young people would want. They might feel very happy and comfortable in a special school setting and might feel going into a mainstream setting very scary and not want to do it. How much are young people able to express their own opinions? Can a child or young person really make an informed choice about which school they attend? It depends on the young person; when you are fourteen, what do you want out of a school? A lot of kids want a group of friends that they get on with and to have a good time. But there are some kids who want to study Maths and English and go on to be stockbrokers. Young people would assess the school for different purposes depending on their priorities. You do need a strong support framework to educate all young people in an inclusive school community.

'A young person attending a special school and taught by staff who understand and value them is more part of an inclusive community than they would be when located in a mainstream school and being viewed as a problem or a difficult person. Inclusion is about being wanted and valued for being you, so if mainstream schools do not have the capacity to alter their provision they will not be able to create an inclusive school community.'

STORIES FROM HEALTH PRACTITIONERS

Julie, speech and language therapist

'I was always interested in communication, in medical aspects of life, the science side, but as I got older I shifted to language and linguistics. At sixteen I wanted to work with people. I was interested in science and medicine and wanted to contribute, to do something useful. I achieved some A-levels in science and then did sociology and English A-levels, which I enjoyed. One of my tutors knew of speech therapy and said she could see me working in that area. My mother had been to a group and had heard a speaker from MENCAP [UK learning disability charity] who said we needed more speech therapists. That was my guiding path. I have never regretted it. I thought I would work with adults but took a job in paediatrics and have always worked with children

'When I first qualified I worked in a clinic in a needy, small town. There was a school two hundred yards from the clinic. I sent out the appointments but the children often failed to arrive, so I walked around to the school and asked if I could see children in the school. The head [teacher] was delighted. I thought if the parents can come along, that would be good, but if not, at least I can work with the school. It was quite revolutionary at the time. From that time I have always liked working in schools. Recent protocols suggest that first referrals are seen in a clinic but I feel many school–age children are more suitably seen in school, which is a familiar environment for them. There is often an educational, language development issue making accessing the curriculum problematical.

'The requirements for linguistic skills may be changing with our screen-orientated society. Language norms could go down with the emergence of TV, computer games, iPads. We are at another sea change so the ability to communicate verbally could even decrease. When I first qualified there were a huge range of special schools and any child who did not hit the norm would be in a special school. Children who had moderate learning difficulties were in special schools. Now inclusion law is such that every child has the right to be educated in mainstream, a complete shift in another direction. For many this is good, but you cannot make one size fit all as children are so different: some need a small specialist environment and others thrive with other children as role models who can do things that they cannot.

'My role as a speech and language therapist [SLT] is primarily clinical work with school children aged from five to sixteen with more emphasis on the primary end, but I like working with older children. I work in mainstream schools, health centres, nurseries and spend a session a week with children in a residential behaviour, emotional, social difficulties [BESD] school. We call it clinical work as we are in a health service, but speech and language therapy is closer to education, "remedial education" as it was years ago, than clinical work. It is intervention. There are some children with specific problems in speech, language and communication (SLC) who are not able to access the curriculum and therefore not included in everything. From an educational perspective they need to access the same curriculum for equal opportunity, but from a health perspective there are certain children who need more help in some areas and there may be some areas of education that are just not appropriate. Communication needs may deny access unless there is significant differentiation.

'From a health perspective we want as many children as possible to have sufficient language to interact as a human being, make relationships, to socialise and to use communication at a primary level which is generally sufficient for everyday adult activities. The needs beyond that are educational needs, really, rather than personal needs. Most adults can cope with an average tabloid [news paper] at eight- or nine-year-old language and reading level. You need a higher level of more abstract, academic language in order to achieve at GCSE, A-level and university level.

'Much of our work is talking about classroom strategies with teachers, ensuring that young people can understand what is being said in the classroom. If they are not understanding new concepts and new topics, you have to go back and explore the new vocabulary and ensure that they understand everything that is needed. For example, if you have to understand "waterproof", there are a number of underlying concepts if a child is going to be involved in that topic.

'Evidence suggests that you can effect more change in expressive language difficulties rather than receptive comprehension. That may be because language understanding involves cognitive factors such as auditory and working memory that may be more intransigent parts of a child's makeup; they cannot change. A lot of comprehension work may take place in the early years – building up their memory, listening and attention and ability to understand instructions of increasing length. As they get older, you may have to recognise that this person may always have difficulty following lengthy instruction, following continuous material and conceptualising abstract vocabulary. It becomes necessary to introduce different teaching strategies; for example, chunking utterances, visual support, written support, use of sign and experiential learning.

'Inclusion is about adjusting the environment rather than the child, so that the young person is helped to access the curriculum. We want to ensure that as many children as possible can access the curriculum, can get what is helpful from the curriculum that is offered and are enabled to benefit from the educational environment. I think our curriculum and view of education are very linguistically biased. Society tends to give more weight to occupations that require high language skills.

'Someone who re-routes a heating system or puts a good joint on a roof is not regarded with as much kudos as someone who has a Classics degree from Cambridge University, but you could argue he is just as essential and as important in life. As a society we tend to revere academic qualifications more than essential life expertise. I would support a concept of inclusion which meant that, within any school environment, both those types of learning could be included on an equal basis.

'We work primarily with education; most Statements of Educational Need include a speech and language report, and the majority of the tribunals are around speech and language or communication or autism. We receive many referrals from paediatricians for a child who may have a social and communication disorder. We observe the child and assess their language skills. We offer support for the school and hopefully contribute to their inclusion in school to ensure the school is able to understand their needs. If there are specific areas to focus on, the LSA may be the person who implements a programme of activities. There is pressure to have more assistants. Language underpins education so that you cannot have education without language so much of our work is carried out by education.

'I give advice on classroom strategies and help staff to understand the impact of SLC (Speech, Language and Communication) needs. We give individual or more formal training for LSAs. Funds for training of education staff are under constraint but we see this as an essential part of an effective service. The therapist works in schools. An approach that has worked well has been where a therapist has focused on the training of one or two LSAs. This has been developed skills and resources to set up groups that target attention, listening, vocabulary development and social skills for children. LSAs have regular sessions with the therapist to train and direct them so that by the end of a year they have developed a set of skills, activities and resources. Financial cuts affect both health and education resources. Schools may choose to buy in more SLT intervention and buy in more therapy if they wish.

'SLTs work with pre-school children and their parents, which includes parent–child interaction: the parent is videoed and aspects of their communication to help the child are discussed. This will involve playing, commenting and involving their child. Parents vary as to how easily and naturally they talk and play with their child.

'Children with significant emotional and behavioural issues are a challenge. If they are disruptive or too difficult to manage they may not be included. Grouping children together who have issues in their upbringing or emotional development is not always the best environment. They may be best helped in small groups (e.g. PRUs [Pupil Referral Units]); one-to-one teaching and sensitive building of relationships may be essential to an environment where they can thrive, to give them stability and awareness that people care for them.

'I feel you cannot say one size fits all; autistic children are so individual. Some do well in a school with good role models and children who can make allowances and understand them. Others need a school with limited distraction, quiet, the classic autistic unit with small classes, clear boundaries, a structured agenda, as that is what suits them. I think some autistic children can cope very well in a mainstream environment as long as the school day appears reasonable and logical and when boundaries are clear for them. Some autistic children cope better with school because they like it when their education becomes more structured and formal.'

Lindsey, occupational therapist

'I was always interested in what motivates people to do well in an organisation. I knew I did not want to teach or go into nursing. My mother recognised that I was a practical sort of person and my Saturday job was working in a hospital for disabled children who were in residential care. This led me to pursue advice about occupational therapy [OT] which I applied for and got in. I found college hard, as it was not making baskets and weaving but a lot of anatomy and psychology. It was a very academic course but I applied myself. Our anatomy teacher said you only learn something well if you have to teach someone else. I remember teaching about the knee joint to another student. I have never forgotten the experience. I achieved the diploma and went out working as an occupational therapist. I met patients and enjoyed this; I could do something that changed people's lives.

'I worked with adults first and then children. I did not have a lot of paediatric training but got a job at a children's hospital seven years after I qualified. In my previous work experience I had developed an ability to understand parents' experiences when their child had difficulties. My employers recognised I could learn about child development through reading books and going on courses whereas being empathetic with parents is dependent on experience. So I got the job and I learnt a lot from observing the children.

'Occupational therapy is looking at the child's functional ability and taking into consideration the limitations of their impairment. We have a medical training and are taught the functional impairments of disability and how this impacts on the child's life. OT is about activity and occupation, so for a child, that's being able to play, learning to dress independently and going to school. OT is dual training, physical disability and psychiatry, and we often do assessments liaising with CAMHS [Child and Adolescent Mental Health Services], who advise where there is a breakdown in parenting skills. For example, handwriting has many stages; some children need to go back in the process to develop foundation skills, knowledge of letter formation. Sometimes more is expected than the child is capable of achieving, particularly if they have missed out on vital stages.

'You may have the more able child with cerebral palsy in a mainstream school, but a teacher does not really know how this impacts on their learning. The occupational therapist assesses the child, how they learn, and identifies the limitations of their impairment. I help the teacher to understand about perception and how to break down things into manageable chunks so the child can learn. The less able children are in special school. Recently there have been funds for occupational therapists to work in special schools.

'People do not always understand what OT is about, as it only came into being after the Second World War. In 1998 we piloted the role of the occupational therapist in a special school to show the team aspects of our work, for example how a supportive chair helps a child sit upright so they can concentrate on holding a pencil to write. During this time I met a micro-technology adviser who showed me what was possible with the use of technology. I learnt how to adapt a toy so the child could play with it and was introduced to software like Clicker, which assists with the development of numeracy and literacy skills. With technology a child can learn to be more independent and empowered. If you enable a child to use a powered wheelchair early on in life they can become more independent and less dependent on their carers from an early stage.

'My role is in transition at the moment; I have three occupational therapists to lead in a newly formed locality service. We each have [responsibility for] named schools as we need to identify with our local population and think about the needs of the children. In this first year we have done in-house training for the SENCO [special educational needs coordinator] cluster groups, working collaboratively looking at ways of working together within our respective organisations. Education and health run parallel to each other and I am keen to break across bureaucratic barriers. The inset training put occupational therapists into the world of education and through the workshop approach we enquired what they wanted from us. I am keen to achieve inclusive working together but feel up against procedures I have to follow, constraints of the national curriculum and lack of resources. By nature, occupational therapists are problem solvers; we use clinical reasoning and attempt to deliver what benefits the child and their family in the most cost-effective way. We are referred children with motor learning difficulties along with physical impairment and aspects of social deprivation.

'I want to use my clinical knowledge to advocate for children at grass-roots level, sharing knowledge rather than ticking boxes. Some children do not have integrated sensory systems and have a significant degree of difficulty with processing sensory information from the environment, for example visual, auditory and tactile stimuli. We use a sensory processing model to understand the behaviours of children with autistic spectrum disorder; for example, we try to help teachers understand that a child is chewing a pencil because he needs to chew on something in order to attend to what the teacher is saying – if the pupil is asked to put his pencil down, it will make it harder for him. We would like to do some training for teachers to give basic ideas to try in the classroom and the more complex cases be referred to occupational therapists.

'The link to attachment disorders presents similar difficulties: this type of child often has difficulty with processing touch. We are pioneering work with CAMHS colleagues to be clear if a child is coming into CAMHS because he has emotional problems or these are secondary to underlying motor difficulties and the child is behaving badly to cover these up. You have to determine whether it is "sensory" or is it "behaviour"?

'We continue to improve our assessment in order to promote our profession and justify what we do. We see children with motor difficulties and then create a programme which usually is implemented by the LSAs. They are brilliant to work with because they know individual children well and see them every day. I do not know their level of knowledge, what their backgrounds are and the type of training they are given. Creating an individual programme takes about two hours and we then rely on the SENCO to pass this on so some minimal training is provided by OT.

'We get a referral, for example, to see a child with autistic spectrum disorder and ask the parent and teacher to complete a sensory profile questionnaire. We score it and it gives us some idea about sensory seeking, low arousal, what activities the child seeks, what they avoid. We then use this to give strategies. We see the child in the environment where they have to function, the classroom, and also talk to the teacher. We have to empower people to see what they are observing. It is about watching. These are the skills I would like to talk to teachers or LSAs about.

'As a profession we need to build up relationships so that teachers are able to meet with us. As an occupational therapist you have to have a "will do" work ethic. OT is about assessment, defining the problem and the solution. I do not give out test results but say a more detailed report is available. It is what you do about it that counts and we do it by a combination of assessment and teaching. I am supporting a colleague applying for a research grant to pay for an OT post to look into the effectiveness of the advice we provide and how services could be used in the future. We need to make time to look at good practice and use a research grant to pay for this time.

'I think inclusion is about empowering a child to learn in an environment with their peer group. It is not taking a child out of the classroom and giving them one-to-one. It is about looking at a child's specific learning needs, looking at the demands of the curriculum and at how you can adapt that to enhance the way a child learns. By definition there are children who cannot be taught in the same way as other children, so they need some modified intervention. Inclusion is enabling a child to think for themselves, but knowing when to give support to help them over learning something. The LSA has a hard job maintaining a balance between providing support and fostering independent learning.

'Children are more complex now, with many different problems, and are doing well getting into mainstream schools. Some special schools seem to be able to deal with the national curriculum in the morning and then in the afternoon be a bit more creative by putting children together who learn in a certain way – mixing year groups up, teaching pupils in an integrated way, incorporating therapy and building upon what children are interested in.

'OT is about function, you need to understand why you are doing something. In training we do a lot of psychology and learn a lot about motivation.

You have to make the task interesting to be worth the effort that goes into doing it. A lot of OT and rehabilitation is getting the child to do an activity they enjoy that gets them to practise the movement you want them to achieve. To practise balance you do not get them to stand on one leg but look at tasks that demand this of a child, such as trampolining. You look at the parents' lifestyle, their economic state and what they do as a family. We work with parents and schools to incorporate activities into the lifestyle of the child. The LSAs may use a visual sequence to encourage the child or use a checklist to remind them to get things out for a particular activity to empower the child to be independent. The LSA helps the child to be independent and develop organizational skills; this is what OT is about.

'When we talk to teachers, we use a developmental model, we talk about how children develop their sensory motor skills so by the time they get to school they should have an integrated system, but some children do not have that. An occupational therapist could assess a child's readiness for learning, which happens in America, where children are taken out for sensory integration therapy, so when they go back to school they have developed some foundation skills. We teach the teacher to consider the developmental stages and building blocks to learning and the children who have missed out some part of the process can benefit from being assessed by an occupational therapist.'

Angela, school nurse

'I have got family members with complex needs, a niece with Down's syndrome who attended a special school where my sister worked as a support worker. I have another niece with really complex needs and severe disabilities. I feel that it is not right for all children to be included but I do have views about accepting children with disabilities. As a society, there is a tendency for people to be embarrassed about people who behave differently, say with autism, and not know how to respond, and by including those children in school environments it makes other children more accepting of them in society. I relate that to my own children and my own nephews and nieces who have got cousins with complex needs and how they have grown up with an acceptance of people with those needs and think nothing of it. My family experiences have influenced my thoughts. My sister is very concerned about the environment where her daughter is as she is very vulnerable. She broke her leg in respite care once because another child sat on her. So from my sister's point of view, a special school environment is a more protective environment.

'The role of the school nurse is moving towards a leadership role within school health, a service for children and young people. Every school has a named nurse but may see different nurses for different reasons. We cannot do exactly what schools want as every year the service outcomes are agreed between our employer and the PCT [Primary Care Trust] in a document.

We are guided by the Healthy Child Programme for school-aged children, school nurses contribute to this as a gold standard. We have to prioritise child protection so we do more of that in some areas – case conference meetings, seeing children, liaising with school and the other professionals involved. The other big thing is immunisation sessions. We immunise against HPV, which is the Human Papilloma Virus, which causes cervical cancer, since 2009 for twelve-year-old girls. It involves three vaccines a year for a course; that was something new for schools to get to grips with. We are also guided by current health needs – obesity is a big one, weight management and a lot of monitoring. We are contracted to provide a weekly drop-in session for secondary-aged children; take-up is varied and some schools involve the Brook sexual health nurse and youth workers, so we liaise with them.

'We take referrals from everybody – families, parents, schools and other professionals. A large part of our work is mental health work tier 1 and tier 2 before CAMHS; engagement is the difficult thing, so we work to get a child engaged in the service. I work in both primary and secondary with a lot of emotional and behavioural things. A lot of issues relating to parenting we now do not simply refer to CAMHS or the community paediatrician, we have to follow criteria. We do an assessment, and if we think that changes to parenting would help we recommend routes for the parents. Parents' hackles go up if you mention attending parenting groups for many reasons, but there are not many groups available so it is not that easy to access if they wished to attend.

'We support schools for children with complex medical needs through their care plans – severe asthma, epilepsy, heart condition, severe allergies that need Epipen. The diabetic children go to the diabetic nurses as this condition changes as the child grows and they understand it better, so they liaise with the schools directly. The emergency care plans where a photo for each child must be accessible to all staff in school, this raises challenges. I find that there are different feelings about confidentiality here: the staff and how they feel, their attitudes is a big one.

'Staff in schools have training for giving medicines in school. On a school trip they have to have someone who can administer medicines for each group of children. We do training sessions for school staff on use of Epipens and epilepsy. PSHE [personal, social, health and economic education] is a big one; we are guided by the commission as to what we can and cannot do. We no longer do sessions on puberty for schools so their staff have to do this now, but we can contribute to the Healthy Child Programme – obesity, key public health issues such as sexual health, obesity, smoking, drug and alcohol use are increasingly becoming target areas. Mental health has been one, but actually at the moment it is not a priority but we are fighting to keep that on. School health assistants monitor growth and development. In the National Child Measuring Programme, every Reception and Year 6 child is measured and their height and weight input into a computer to work out their BMI [body mass index], and if they are obese a letter goes to the parent. A lot of controversy about this.

'I work in a complex of three schools: a secondary, a primary and a special school. The majority of my work is picking up referrals – child protection cases, children with needs: mental health needs, emotional and behavioural problems, autistic children and social issues that impact on the development of the child. We support some with physical health needs. We have a direct line through to Social Services so a lot of liaison takes place with social workers. We are a three-way link – school, social workers and school nurses. It is usually us three sitting round the table together communicating information between social workers and education. We are always saying we need social workers in schools, we have police. I often say that teachers are not just teachers, they are social workers too. My colleague in child protection at school will say "Are you going to the meeting?" so we check on each other and share information and support each other. I do not give clinical supervision but it is good to talk with someone about some of these cases. You subconsciously are supporting each other in some of these cases.

'It is important for us as school nurses to have a key link with school. It is hard to access them sometimes to have time to talk to each other. They have such busy lives as they are so stretched.

'My thoughts on inclusion are around the children with complex and medical needs and their inclusion into the wider school community. The children with emotional and behavioural issues are of concern to me because I do see across the board that those children cannot cope in mainstream. I see the transitions, from reception all the way through, and often I see the path. It is sad when you see them lost. Including children of different ages within the school community raises issues of diversity and equality. I have come across good and bad examples of inclusion. I met a boy who had been found on a container ship, he only spoke Swahili. He was new into the country with all the unmet health needs as there is no screening in his home country. Often children may have hearing and sight problems that have not been picked up. However, the Catholic secondary school where this lad went tried very hard to make him part of the community.

'Emotional and behavioural issues are a big one – I see a lot of children who come and talk to me. I am the middle person and they talk to me about what is not fair. It feels as if they get themselves a label and so if they are anywhere near an incident they get the blame. When I see these children who have a lot of baggage I feel that their perspective is quite sad. Some schools work really hard to include them and then it still fails and sometimes it is fantastic to see the children who have gone through. Moving from permanent exclusion to coping in the mainstream school environment and included, because of the support they have had. They might have had a referral through to the paediatrician and been medicated and that has helped them with their education; this can work. I have seen children that have struggled and failed and witnessed the frustrations of a child with high level of need not recognised and not getting the support they need in mainstream school.

'The design of the school is important. One new school I work within can see everyone – the toilets open out into school and the hand washing facilities open into the corridor. Bullying takes place in toilets so this has worked well, as in the old school, children would be round corners distressed. The design of the school has made it a less threatening environment. When I first went into a secondary school you had to walk the corridors with "attitude" otherwise you would be pressed against the wall. I was an adult and it took getting used to, so what is it like for a young person? The openness, they have got no narrow corridors, the layout of the school is easier to find where you have to go to, and the teachers' offices have got glass windows so you can see if there is anyone in there. You can find the person you are looking for easily, not all hidden away; there is always someone around. It is less threatening for them. As a school nurse, I do not work in the environment all day but look at it with different eyes from a teacher.

'The environment is key: the design and the fact that a well-maintained, well-designed building sends a message out that everyone is valued. There is a lot of controversy among the staff about the space they work in, but a strong emphasis on behaviour has had a major impact. The strict uniform, the structured discipline regime, the very clear behaviour policy work well. There is an internal exclusion policy so children who are excluded still have to come into school and stay in one classroom. They are not allowed out for dinner or break but are segregated from the rest of the school. This classroom is staffed well for children with behavioural difficulties – ten children in the class.

'In my experience, a Catholic school has clear governance within it. I may not believe the views, but the workings of the school staff demonstrate a caring ethos, a community with equal caring for everyone. I can pick up on the ethos as a visitor to the school because they welcome me as part of their team, fantastic staff.

'From a health perspective, what worries us as school nurses is inclusion for children with medical needs where staff perspectives and attitudes on issues lead them to not take responsibilities. We find staff not wanting to do first aid, or give medicines, or engage with Epipen training. My thoughts are that if you were in a situation, you would feel guilty if you did nothing, so at least you know something about allergic responses, to do the basics. I think staff are afraid of doing something wrong, not understanding; they have so much pressure on them. Usually it is the support staff who deal with the medical needs but we still need the odd teacher able to act as you cannot guarantee support staff always being there. Disabled children in wheelchairs are in mainstream now, they get around the school building. There is a child in a wheelchair with funding for one-to-one support from a LSA. He has not come to me at all, a great sign; he has a group of kids around him and seems fine. There was a Down's girl in the secondary school who needed a lot of input, but she was accepted well into the school. She looked different but the Catholic ethos was accepting. They have been bringing children across from the special school and it is that acceptance of the pupils and the staff of being used to children who are different being amongst them. Children can be very accepting of each other if you develop that early on in the community. The pupils from secondary ages go into the special school and help in the nursery, as well the girls who are doing childcare.

'The student support centre has a maximum of thirty learners. One lad had real problems with anger in mainstream, always in trouble, and one day he talked to me. He said he could not cope with the big classes and did not know what to do as he felt safer in the small class and knew he could not cope in the big classes. Another example of a boy with autism: when the school was operating a more relaxed curriculum for a week he could not cope. He was unchaining his bike to go home; he could not stay as he knew he would lose it. He had learned to manage his responses, but in a more open curriculum he could not cope, so he went home. One family had two girls with autism, very difficult social skills. Now in Years 9 to 10, one of the girls is amazing, she smiles all the time – she has learned to do this, she talks to me now, and she is doing hairdressing and is a brilliant example of how an inclusive school can include a young person with autism.

'It works for some, it does not work for all; they are all individual. With all the money in the world you could tailor to each child but you could not change everything about the school environment, so I do not know what the answer is. As a school nurse I contribute to inclusion and yes, it can be fantastic, but there are always children for whom it will not work.'

THE AUTHORS' STORIES AND REFLECTIONS

Diana's story

'I was born in Bulgaria in the middle of its communist period, when people were believers in the progressive society they were destined to build. Life was basic, secure, collective and enjoyable. There are two major traditions that run through my family history. On one side there is a long-lasting commitment to and professional involvement in education, starting with my great grandfather, one of the first graduates of the pedagogic faculty at the Bulgarian University in 1893. Subsequently, there is a long list of relatives who belong to the teaching profession: teachers, sports teachers and head teachers. On the other side, my ancestors were revolutionaries – active in the fight against fascism, and in the socialist revolution for a more just society.

'When I was growing up, my mother was head teacher of a technical college. When I started school she had decorated every one of my notebooks with a different proverb emphasising the value of hard work, study for progress and success, research and education. In both pre-school and primary school I learned that academic achievement features very high in our culture. Communist slogans read "from everyone depending on their ability, to everyone according to their need". Communist education was about developing all-rounded individuals. Education aimed to create opportunities for all pupils' physical, mental, spiritual, moral and creative development, according to their potential.

'At the age of fourteen I moved to a German language school as I was interested to study foreign languages and cultures. The first year was dedicated to learning German, and in the remaining four years education was carried out predominantly in the German language, where possible with native German teachers from the former GDR [German Democratic Republic]. Often these teachers had more a relaxed attitude and acceptance of students' sub-culture than their Bulgarian counterparts.

'I started school a month later than everybody else because of ill health. Initially, it was hard for me because all my class mates had already acquired a thousand fluent conversational words in German. After some time, however, I finally caught up and rapidly climbed up to the top of the class. The breakthrough came when I was called out in front of the class to recite a poem about the musicians of Bremen. Instrumental to the process of bringing me up to a higher level was my pairing up with one of the best achievers in the class in the German language. Looking back, I think the breakthrough came as a direct result of this Vygotskian social constructivist learning, which included negotiation of knowledge, scaffolding and, last but not least, a developing friendship.

'I was brought up with the values of collectivism, collaboration, cohesion, patriotism, friendship and peace. I was brought up to believe that every member of society should be valued equally, irrespective of the type of contribution they could offer to society. I also learnt that this meant every member who wasn't against the system, or whose abilities did not deviate from the "norm" to such an extent that they would be regarded as misfits. Such unfortunate people lived mostly in isolation but the system provided for them according to their perceived deviant needs.

'Defectology came to Bulgaria at university level in the early 1980s as a welcome regular Soviet science import; it came to me in a letter from the university with an offer for a student place. The new university qualification "defectology" was open for student enrolment in 1983. Defectologists were going to be trained to work in special schools and in clinical practice. The first cohort of twenty-four students, including myself, commenced training in September of 1984.

'These developments followed the publication of L.S. Vygotsky's collected works in Moscow in the early 1980s, amongst which volume five was entitled *Foundations of defectology* [Vygotsky 1983]. Defectology, following Vygotsky's example, was studied in a truly interdisciplinary fashion. He believed that where there is a complex interplay between the biological, functional and social, there is a need for an interdisciplinary approach to its study. Although marked by the dominant epistemology and the deficit language of its time, Vygotsky's work endorsed the idea that the social influence has a determining role on individual outcomes.

'In these early days, defectology in Bulgaria captured Vygotsky's legacy for interdisciplinary study. It was defined as a separate "scientific discipline" with its distinct "subjects" and "objects" of enquiry. Yet the social influences so clearly credited by Vygotsky were hardly explored in the studies. Social influences were studied as far as the micro and meso systems [Bronfenbrenner 1979] are concerned and never reached anywhere near the macro-structural, societal and – God forbid! – the political.

'Defectology was constructed as a science about the peculiarities in the physical and mental development of handicapped children and the law-like regularities of their instruction, education and schooling [Dobrev 1992]. The implication was that children's "defects" were an object of interdisciplinary study and also that there are "law-like regularities in their education" that need to be discovered and used to advantage. The core concepts of defectology were "correction", "compensation" and "rehabilitation". The latter was understood as a development in the general direction of the "norm". Initially, the foundational two years of teacher preparation consisted of medical, psychological, philosophical, foundational pedagogic and linguistic modules. The upgrade included methodologies of teaching curriculum subjects to different categories of handicapped students. There was ongoing practice, predominantly limited to observations, and a final school experience consisting of three months' direct teaching. The acquired knowledge had to be applied to practice alongside learning from experienced teachers how to deliver calibrated lessons. In the case of teaching the intellectually handicapped, this calibration included reduction of curriculum contents, slower pace of teaching, problem solving and use of some access strategies (use of adequate visualisation, multi-sensory approaches to teaching and learning).

'In my second year at university, eleven out of the twenty-four students of defectology on my course dropped out to move to courses that offered better social prospects like law, languages, journalism, etc. I graduated with the remaining thirteen in 1988 as a teacher of the intellectually handicapped with a second speciality in speech therapy, which, at the time, was conceptualised as a pedagogical discipline.

'In 1988, I graduated successfully with a Diploma in Higher Education that was equivalent to a combination of BA and MA degrees. Until February 1989 I worked as a teacher in a special pre-school centre for children with severe communication difficulties. I took responsibility for a class of learners with severe stuttering and stammering. During this time I began to question the specialness of my pedagogy and the purpose of educating this group of children in a segregated setting. I was determined to expand on my knowledge through research and in 1989 I embarked upon a full-time PhD in the area of intellectual handicap.

'My PhD research was heavily influenced by Vygotsky's theory and by his followers in the USSR, namely A.I. Ivanova and V.I. Lubovsky. They built on Vygotsky's theory about the zone of proximal development and on his theory about the relationship between language and thought in cognitive functioning. I explored their work on learning potential that was perceived as an important indicator for intellectual functioning in children, and as a predictor for future educational achievement. Subsequently I connected these ideas to others' work about dynamic assessment and scaffolding. There were clear implications for the practice of identification, categorisation and school placement of children labelled as intellectually handicapped. There was recognition in the home literature [Dobrev 1979, 1984] at the time that some children, and arguably groups of children, were often wrongly identified as intellectually disabled and were subsequently placed in special schools. My PhD research aimed to make a contribution in this area by emphasising the role of education and pedagogy (facilitation and scaffolding) in intellectual functioning and by arguing for dynamic assessment designs to surpass the limitations of "static" assessment, mainly through intelligence testing. The hope was that this would bring about change to identification and educational practices.

'In 1989, Bulgaria officially parted with communism. This created new opportunities to break free from isolation and explore the world beyond the Iron Curtain.

'I visited the UK for the first time in 1990. My personal contacts with academics from the UK led to the formulation of a proposal for a joint

European initiative in teacher education. The aim was to restructure teacher education practices for SEN through the utilisation of a reflective practice approach. In 1992, I also started a career as a teacher educator at the University of Sofia.

'Continuous efforts to make international collaboration possible paid off: after a few years of unsuccessful submissions to the European Commission (EC) we finally succeeded in securing the grant of approximately £300,000 to be spent over a three-year period for exchange visits and development activities. The EC Tempus project entitled Action on Reflective Practice [see Tzokova and Garner, 1996] was the first of its kind: a large international initiative aiming to restructure teacher education practices in Bulgaria. It commenced in 1994 and was given an additional extended year until it was fully completed in 1998. At this time I met Jane Tarr, who participated in the project.

'As a result of the international co-operation and exchange, a considerable shift in thinking, awareness of the necessity for change and consequent action were marked in all aspects of defectology and teacher education in Bulgaria. One of the immediate effects was that in 1994 defectology as a university speciality was renamed as "special education". This change was brought about by an understanding having developed about the crucial role education played in the field of disabilities. This represented an attempt to move away from the predominantly medical and psychological "deficit" focus that defectology adopted in Bulgaria towards looking at education as a critical means to bring about change for disabled children and young people. The change, although seemingly linguistic at first, resulted from the cross-cultural exploration of teacher education and school practices with disabled children, alongside professional reflection in project participants. During the development exchange project we visited both mainstream and special schools in the UK, studied literature and observed, and took away a lot of reflections and materials. We explored the concepts of SEN and integration as proposed on the basis of the Warnock Report [1978] and were able to see how this has been implemented in schools.

'My colleagues and I changed the way we thought and saw our own practice: a change that, albeit difficult to grasp or measure, over time came to shape subsequent developments in the special education field in Bulgaria. The fact that the project included all teacher educators from the defectology departments of the two major universities in this country was very important. Colleagues were enabled to reflect and learn together and the impact of such an approach carried an undoubtedly more sustainable promise. In those days, though, defectology never came to be fully and critically deconstructed. I believe there was an aspiration to learn from and acquire "better" models of theory and practices without a full engagement or contemplation of their meaning within our context. Although defectology was renamed "special education", the existing categories of disabilities continued to frame the field. Teacher education adopted some new courses and titles, amongst them one named "integrated education"; however, the structures remained unchallenged and preserved.

'One of the most tangible results of the EC Tempus project included the creation of the *Bulgarian Journal of Special Education* in 1995, which I founded and edited in its first years. The journal aimed to bring academics and practitioners in this field closer together and served as a platform for discussions and popularisation of the renamed field of "special education". The project had an enormous impact on me both personally and professionally. As the coordinator, I was involved in the running of it over the years but also worked closely with both the national and international groups of participants. Working together with a common purpose in familiar and unfamiliar environments was not only illuminating but also promoted trust and a bond between individuals and groups.

'Personally, I found the whole international experience fascinating and inspiring. I began to wonder about how we learn from such experiences and how then change can be enabled. I wanted to learn more, to explore more and to try and make sense of these processes. I was also eager to get to know the UK cultural, social and educational context in more depth.

'Personal circumstances and continuous professional contacts with colleagues from the UK created this opportunity for me, and towards the end of the joint project, in 1996, I moved to the UK to engage in a piece of research for a second PhD. My aim was to continue the process of cross-cultural learning that has opened up a lot of questions and opportunities for me. My research confirmed the hunch that despite the noble aims, the enthusiasm and the promises, little has actually changed in our higher education or "special education" practices six years on from the beginning of the project. These findings led me to question the what, how and why of international exchange and comparative research, and to look for explanations of a more philosophical, social and cultural and, more importantly, global and political nature. My work has been further informed by teaching responsibilities for a CPD [continuing professional development] programme in special education in the UK, related to the education of children with severe, profound and multiple learning difficulties, and by a direct engagement in one special school over two years.

'In 2000, new developments interrupted my personal and professional life course. The CPD programme in Severe Learning Difficulties that I was teaching was discontinued. My research work was interrupted before I managed to complete it. The rule of immigration control was uncompromising. I had to make very quick decisions. I either had to make quick arrangements to stay in the UK as a self-employed person or I had to go back home to my work at the Bulgarian University.

'I decided to stay in the UK and to give up my university career. I can say my decision was more instinctive than rational. Looking back, I try to rationalise about it but the truth is at the time I just plunged in. The following years were marked by a lot of practical difficulties to do with immigration: rules, regulations, restrictions, emotional turmoil and the beginning of my journey alongside what is being labelled as autism. This abrupt change has had a tremendous impact on my personal and professional development.

'A close friend of mine has already worked in applied behaviour analysis within home-based early intervention programmes. We had discussions about it, I visited a workshop and, although I had great reservation about the nature and method of these programmes, I was tempted to explore it first hand and to meet and get to know the children. So I started working with one child, then another and another and so it became my main occupation. I worked with children and young people labelled as autistic between 2000 and 2006. The children I worked with followed the programmes from an early age (in some instances as young as two to three years of age) and subsequently went to mainstream schools with a personal shadow. I also worked in schools and with school staff to try to see opportunities for adaptations that would enable successful education of these children in mainstream schools. I loved the children. My contact with them was very intensive and I ended up spending up to forty hours a week with up to four children at a time. I worked with some of them until they were ten or eleven and still now keep in touch as a friend. Quite a large part of this work took place in mainstream primary schools in London. Most of the time, schools were unable to adapt and include these children. The onus was on the children to change and fit in, and if they failed to do so they were excluded. Some adaptations were made and some schools and teachers were better than others, but overall I continued to see and experience attempts at assimilation and not inclusion.

'The influence of this work on me has been profound. I felt very angry and I struggled with the overpowering control and exclusion, and more often than not with futile efforts to change rigid structures. I wanted to critically scrutinise and expose the conditions that perpetuated exclusion and to delve deeper into the question of what needs to be done to enable real change in education that could lead to more inclusive frameworks and practices. I also thought about my own contribution and responsibility for exclusion.

'I returned to academic work in order to rebuild my confidence and to give myself time to unpack some "bundles", reflect on my experiences and continue to ask questions and find answers. I taught for two years at Sofia University and tried to raise awareness, to see and share a critical picture of autism in relation to educational practices. Having been out of academia for a while, I needed to catch up with the latest research and theory in the area of inclusive education.

'Bulgaria became a member of the European Union in 2007 and as such was under external pressure to demonstrate levels of social and educational practices with regard to disability and inclusion compatible with the other member countries. Educational legislation aimed at reforms in the traditional parallel systems of special and mainstream education was already underway. Practical implementation became a focus of debate with increasing participation of different educational stakeholders. I was actively involved in these debates through publications [Tsokova 2002, 2007a and b, 2008, 2009, 2010] examining current trends in the national and international contexts of inclusive education, exploring existing barriers and looking at future opportunities.

'In 2008, I took part, together with Jane, in an ERASMUS project (ERASMUS Intensive Programme: Educational contributions to building cohesion within European social and institutional life (2008–2009)). I led a number of Bulgarian special education and social work students on a two-week intensive programme in Latvia. With our students we explored European contributions to social cohesion and inclusion. My experience in Latvia was formative and unforgettable. The structure and organisation of the programme activities were designed to create within the international group the very processes that we aimed to explore on the outside. It was a very intense emotional and social experience resulting in lasting connections and friendships. Student participants from various countries continue to keep in touch with each other and with me.

'Since 2008, I have worked as a teacher educator for SEN and inclusive education in ITT [initial teacher training] and CPD in the UK. I have worked not only with student teachers, but also with professionals from very diverse international and disciplinary backgrounds. I have supervised educational psychologists' doctoral studies. My work has been very challenging and exciting.

For the first time, I have tried to truly connect my personal history with my professional practical experience. I have explored theories, policy and research and I have talked to people.

'I believe inclusion develops as a personal and professional process. I would agree with Azzopardi [2008] that it is difficult to distinguish between the two: it is about understanding, valuing and living with difference; it is about self-knowledge, expression and relationships, participation and citizenship, and about equity. I can see that inclusion in this sense is also about education and the kind of pedagogy that would enable it.

'The writing of this book has prompted me to explore my personal biography at a level that I have not done before. It has also given me an opportunity to talk to and listen to a diverse group of people whom I have met in the course of my life and the interaction with whom I have found illuminating and enriching.'

Diana's reflections

'I do not wish to start theorising about how one becomes passionate about inclusive education. I can only think of it through the experiences I have had – personal and professional. Throughout my life, I have experienced a variety of ways of learning: some born out of a wide range of cultural and cross-cultural influences and encounters; some acquired by acceptance of the dominant ideology, theoretical or pedagogical approaches followed by their deconstruction and critique. The process of reflection has played a significant role, as have reading, thinking and spontaneous action. I have drawn on my own instincts and intuition and I am aware of my constant urge and tendency to theorise, to find answers, to be sure.

'Contradiction and doubt can be powerful influences as well. Knowledge can develop through instincts, intuition, imagination and perceptiveness – processes much less prone to rationalisation. I now realise that arguably the most significant role in the shaping of my views about inclusion was played by the feelings of love, interdependence, trust and compassion aided by resilience. I believe it is the unique combination of all of these that has made me question the roots of exclusion, and opened up opportunities and hope for me in relation to inclusion and inclusive education. I realise that on both a personal and a professional level, inclusion is a lifelong process, and I'm determined to try to live it with sensitivity, vigilance and hope.

'The reflection on my own experiences has been the most challenging aspect of the book writing process because of the pain it has brought up. What exactly is my story? Can there be something like "the story" and what is the point? At times I have felt that the story is perhaps more in the things I did not say or could not say because of complex feelings of ethics. I think our stories change constantly. As we move on and learn, we change, and our perspectives change; we may see things in a different light and/or feel empowered to share more with people and thus engage on a deeper level.'

Jane's story

'I was born in a small rural town in Kwazulu Natal, South Africa, as my parents, on getting married, decided to move to Ixopo with my father's teaching work at a secondary school for solely white students, teaching History. In keeping with the social frameworks in South Africa at that time, I was cared for by a Zulu woman named Gervasia and spent my early years playing in our garden with her children and my younger brother and sister. Our friendships were short-lived as the volatile political situation led to the Sharpville massacre [1960] and my father realised that the deep segregation in South African society was not an environment he wished us, as his children, to grow up within. We bid farewell to a beautiful but systemically divided country, separated from my beloved nanny Gervasia and her children, and travelled by ship to England.

'On return to the UK I entered my formal education in a Catholic primary school, in keeping with my parents' religious beliefs. Such schools where members share a religious belief often promote a powerful community ethos and work hard to include those with physical, sensory and intellectual chal-lenges, though without heralding "inclusion" as such. I recall several children in my school who found the general educational work challenging for various reasons but we studied, played and ate together within the same setting. An example was when I learned to play the piano playing together with a friend whose sight was severely impaired. I progressed on to an all-girl convent secondary school where my work experience took me into a local special school. I recall being fascinated by a young boy who walked about the classroom apparently disengaged from the activity I was doing with three others at a table. As we concluded the session he went to the misty window, drew a tree with his finger and wrote his name under it – an action that others in the group had found challenging. This display of a different learning process fascinated me at the time.

'On leaving school I embarked on a music degree at university and volunteered each week to lead percussion and singing workshops for adults with learning difficulties living in an isolated residential hospital care setting. I also did babysitting for families of children with disabilities. Both of these voluntary experiences impacted upon my future career, enhancing my interest in people who learned in different ways but giving me insights into the social separation and division that some groups of people experience within society.

'Fascinated by children who find learning hard, I worked part-time as a music teacher in a private special school. I taught piano to a girl with no speech but who took great pleasure in playing harmonies which she recognised, and witnessed her beginning to sing as she played tunes she knew. I began to understand how music could be a pathway for self-expression and emotional experiences for everyone, but particularly for young and old people with so-called learning difficulties or disabilities. My musicianship has often enabled me to communicate with others less socially skilled and has enhanced my principles for social inclusion. Music has the power to connect people, regardless of their differences and has been for me a useful tool for educational and social inclusion [Tarr and Thomas 2000].

'The birth of my daughter and subsequent years as a single parent were challenging but joyful. I was no longer a member of any religious community so the social isolation of being a single parent in the 1970s gave me real experience of exclusion, prejudice and discrimination and developed in me a determination to support my daughter and be independent. Eventually I trained as a teacher and during my final teaching practice with disabled children aged four to seven years, made contact with a local mainstream school, facilitating exchange visits and learning about each others' specific needs and strengths. I recorded the activity for the local newspaper as my first experience of educational and social inclusion in practice and the building of opportunities to be together for children across the learning spectrum.

'My first qualified teaching job was as a class teacher in a residential school for teenage girls with social and emotional difficulties. After one term, we performed Joseph and his Amazing Technicolor Dreamcoat in a local hall, singing and playing recorders to a small audience of enthralled parents, staff and community members. This was a major achievement for these young women, whose self-esteem was greatly enhanced. Such a performance in the locality enabled our neighbours to gain insight into the educational process taking place for these troubled young people living within their community. The young women demonstrating their musicianship within the local community contributed to building social cohesion and inclusion beyond the school, [which is] particularly valuable for special schools.

'Within another special school, groups of children participated in local music events: festivals, competitions with other mainstream schools, singing carols in community homes for the elderly, raising money for local charities through performances and inviting the community to annual school shows. It was through these musical experiences that children and young people were able to develop self-esteem and to some extent recognition and respect within the local community around the school. A group of young people, working through music and movement, developed relationships with several profoundly disabled youngsters from another local special school. Frequent visits from community and college-based musicians and drama groups enabled learners in a then rather mono-cultural location in south-west Britain to engage with Irish, Ghanaian, Japanese, Balinese and Nigerian musicians. Engagement in singing, percussion and playing simple instruments led learners to interact with others in an enjoyable and collaborative manner. This "outreach" work was important in nurturing social relationships in the mainstream community from the potentially isolated location of a special school.

'In 1986, I initiated the Arts Integration Project, which involved special schools working with their local mainstream schools on a devised music theatre piece which was subsequently performed in a local theatre. This project ran in the spring term annually for several years, providing a stimulus for special and mainstream schools to build relationships. Actiontrack, a music theatre group, visited each pair of schools regularly over the spring term, to encourage creation of songs and stories and maintain the impetus and quality of the productions [Tarr 1997].

'I recall one performance in a local theatre talking to the parent of a young woman with cerebral palsy, waiting for the show to start. She said "I never dreamed that I would be coming to the theatre to watch my daughter perform on stage, it is something I will treasure for ever". This was a motivating factor for me to ensure greater awareness in society of the contributions of disabled people so such an experience would not be so unusual for parents. The project established that able peers could benefit from working alongside and sharing their skills with those less capable, providing an illustration of a mutual learning context. This became an important ingredient in my developing argument for inclusive education: that all learners, able-bodied and disabled, benefit from being together for their own learning. The evidence is clear within the performing arts where different contributions can be valued, but relies upon active pedagogical approaches for more academic areas of study.

'In 1988, I moved into higher education where, in the early days, I recall inviting a young adult in to share with trainee teachers his experiences of special school education. He spoke vehemently of his desire to learn to read and how he had never been taught in school. Consequently, he now was attending evening classes in his early adult life to learn to read. This was a disturbing challenge to the preconceptions of special education and resulted in lengthy debate about curriculum and the rights of disabled learners to the same experiences as other learners, at the time when the national curriculum was being introduced across the education system and debate about rights for children was developing [UNCRC 1989].

'At this time, Diana and I met through a European-funded project exploring special education in Bulgaria, UK, Ireland and Greece. Visiting and discussing each other's provision led to a growing interest to share the positive aspects of each experience and enhance social and educational provision for all learners. An emphasis on advocacy for disabled young people to encourage decision-making and independence skills emerged through our recognition of the UNCRC. We continued to work together on a further European project to explore educational approaches for disadvantaged learners, which led to meeting a colleague in Finland who trains social pedagogues. Social pedagogues often work with children and young people with disabilities to provide social and educational experiences where they can learn alongside their more able peers in an inclusive context. The emphasis for social pedagogues is on social aspects of learning which reinforce the educational value of social interaction between able-bodied and disabled learners.

'Embarking on doctoral study renewed my interest in the challenges faced by parents of children with disabilities. I focused upon narrative interviews with parents who communicated their extensive knowledge and skills concerning their children and their frustration in frequent professional disregard for their insights. Interviews with professionals from education, health, social care and the voluntary sector at that time demonstrated limited understanding or sharing across each others' roles and responsibilities, despite their involvement with the same family.

'To ensure that new primary school teachers were aware of diverse learners, we initiated a short special school placement for trainees as part of their QTS [qualified teacher status] programme. In this context, trainees could develop pedagogical skills in differentiation, meet professionals from range of different agencies and extend their communicative competence to a wider range of learners. This opportunity has been available for the past seventeen years for trainee primary teachers.

'The late 1990s saw huge expansion of additional often unqualified adults working in schools to support learners who were the most challenging for the teacher to include. This swiftly growing group of paraprofessionals – teaching and learning assistants – developed their knowledge and skills "on the job" through their empathy and sensitivity to children and family needs. Such adults have become a significant resource for schools in providing for all learners' needs and frequently they work alongside the most vulnerable learners in the education system. In recognition of the educational needs of these paraprofessionals in the late 1990s, I developed programmes of study for teaching and learning assistants – to ensure that learners with special educational needs in mainstream school particularly worked with qualified and perceptive adults. I have found that these professionals were highly motivated to expand their roles and responsibilities in support of more inclusive school communities. Many have progressed into teaching with a heightened insight into the social and educational needs of individual children – a beneficial awareness as a school teacher.

'The policy, *Every Child Matters: Change for Children* [DfES 2004], encouraged educationalists to build closer partnerships with colleagues in social care and health. As a professional trainer for the wider workforce, I developed relationships with colleagues in the conjoining Faculty of Health and Social Care and initiated inter-professional events where trainee teachers, trainee social workers and trainee children's nurses and midwives came together to share their professional aspirations and goals. These events supported trainees in understanding the common goals of professionals for children and young people despite the often very different language and culture which alienated professionals from each other.

'Drawing upon the local community has been a facet of teaching and learning in higher education. Teaching about child protection and safeguarding involved a group of professional practitioners – social workers, police officers, health practitioners and teachers – drawn from the children's workforce collaborating in a multi-disciplinary approach. Together with disabled colleagues, we devised action plans and programmes to educate colleagues in understanding their legal responsibilities to include disabled learners and heighten awareness of respectful ways of developing such provision. More recently we have, across the Faculty of Education with the Faculty of Health and Social Care, written a foundation degree for anyone working with "children, young people and their families" specifically to address the Common Core of Skills and Knowledge [CWDC 2010]. Colleagues in Health and Social Care provide a different perspective on children with disability. Discussion and debate have taken place about how each of us understands "disability" and the demands placed on the training of professionals to work in a socially and educationally inclusive society. Some professionals continue to demand specialised segregated provision for disabled children whilst others can see the challenges and benefits of inclusion and strive for deeper levels of social and educational inclusion.

'Foundation degrees enable those less represented in higher education to engage in further study. Their engagement broadens the knowledge base of higher education, potentially making it a more inclusive vibrant learning environment. Such interest in people who feel excluded from the formal education system led in the early 2000s to my engagement with supplementary schools. These are informal schools organised within communities of various different cultural groups, to provide children and young people with the learning that their parents feel they are not able to receive in formal schooling. The activities, run by volunteers, can focus on religious or cultural knowledge together with activities to develop English language skills, specific ICT skills and the development of young people's confidence and self-esteem. I was invited along with colleagues to devise programmes of study for these volunteers to develop their teaching and learning skills, enable them to build their understanding of the formal education system and support their partnership with mainstream schools in support of their young people. Teachers from mainstream schools visited supplementary schools and enhanced their knowledge of different community groups and increased insight into the social and educational aspirations of the young people in their classrooms. This experience for teachers of working amidst and across sites of learning in the shared intercultural spaces between community and school has the potential for "teachers to develop 'flex identities' of the kind that are currently expected of their pupils as they enter the school premises" [Clough and Tarr 2011].

'My work today seeks to enrich the pedagogy of all phases of education to enable learners to contribute their experiences and insights and to broaden individual learning networks.'

Jane's reflections

'I can now reflect upon a key question: how is it that I have spent so much of my life trying to develop my own personal and professional inclusive practices, what has motivated me to this goal? As I read my story I feel the stark reality of my early experience of separations in South Africa, which remained as painful memories for me until 1993, when the apartheid regime fell, and 1995, when I eventually visited South Africa to be with my estranged nanny Gervasia. I wonder if this early experience has caused me to hold contempt for any systems that separate people – young from old, black from white, disabled from able bodied? I can only think that justification for such separations will look futile and absurd to future generations. Such a position has not led to an easy path for me in the field of education but I am pleased that my story and this brief reflection can sit alongside the stories of others who have committed their energy and skills to develop understanding of inclusive communities.'

Reflection on our learning from our joint experiences

We revisited some of our joint professional experience in order to trace links to our developing ideas. As it is shared in both of our stories, our international joint research initiatives were designed to support social intercultural learning. Our first project in the early 1990s promoted a reflective practice approach to encourage professional development by allowing re-conceptualisation and restructuring of teacher education practices targeted at marginalised learners across a number of European higher education institutions. Our second joint project participation in 2008 in turn took this further in developing a model for cohesive community learning in cross-cultural contexts. Instrumental in this project was the emerging understanding that

> Intercultural dialogue is seen as a dimension in the relationships between the powerful and the less powerful, for example between ethnic minority groups, between voluntary sector and professional workers, between teachers and learners. Intercultural dialogue is seen as potentially making contributions towards understanding difference, solving problems and achieving social cohesion.
>
> (Grundtvig Lifelong Learning Programme: Engaging in intercultural dialogues as a basis for developing programmes in HE 2007–09)

The learning experience on this international intensive programme engaged participants in open and respectful dialogue about their own personal and professional experiences. Together and in diverse groups they re-presented their experiences, engaged in new enterprises and formulated new approaches to problem solving and understanding differences. This rich learning experience resulted in a deeper understanding of diverse world views and practices. In our experience, this learning model produced a lasting effect as individual participants maintained their connection, continued their exploration and developed new ways of networking.

For us, the key is that participation in diverse learning communities of this kind promotes a deeper understanding of learning as a social process enriched by the diversity of the participants and their contributions.

Chapter 3

Discussion of key learning points

The process of collecting the stories in this book and reflecting upon them has led to some key learning points for us. The intellectual and emotional engagement with the people and their stories has enabled us to enhance our understanding of inclusion and inclusive school communities.

Individual contributions

What thoughts did the stories stimulate? What connections have we made? We took something away from each story: sometimes this was something new that neither of us had been aware of before, like details about the contributions of the school nurse, the occupational therapists and the governor within their contexts. We have attempted to understand the context of each contribution and in doing so we gained some further insight about the function of schooling in the wider social and policy context. The reading of the stories reinforced the benefit from knowing through engaging with a wide range of perspectives.

Our initial plan was to collect life stories that illustrated individual experience with education and inclusion and then put them together to enable a starting point for thinking and understanding of inclusive school communities through individual roles and contributions. This gradually shifted to crafting of individual stories from transcripts of conversations around the core questions we had posed to prompt conversation. The structure of the crafted stories led to further framing and insights about the relationships between the components of early life experiences, professional experiences, conceptual understanding of inclusion and the roles, responsibilities and potential contribution to inclusive school communities. We developed a construct map (see Figure 3.1) seeking to represent the relationship between our core concepts and story components.

The social, historical, cultural, and political and educational context for each story is crucially important in enabling understanding of people's experiences, values and struggles and their positioning in relation to inclusion. As Heshusius proposes:

> Learners always bring to the situation their own personal, social, cultural and political histories, purposes, and interpretations, whether we are or are not aware of it or acknowledge it. Learning occurs at various but equally valid levels, including kinaesthetic, intuitive, and nondiscursive.
>
> (Heshusius 2004: 50)

In the UK context, inclusive education has been encouraged through policy initiatives in the last thirty years. However, the inherent contradiction remains that the 'needs' discourse stands in the way of truly transformative education (Armstrong 2005, Armstrong *et al.* 2010; Slee 2011; Florian 2008).

Our continuous engagement with each story from conversation to crafted text prompted reflections and an active discussion about the profound impact of early life experiences on the subsequent personal constructs and positioning of people in relation to difference, inclusion and inclusive school communities. Early experiences and feelings brought about by exclusion, educational marginalisation and inequality appear to impact in different ways in different people. The development of inclusive values and the struggle for their realisation appear to be dependent on the social circle around the person and the levels of compassion, support and encouragement that the person is enabled to draw upon, whether this is from family and extended family, friends, school and wider community members. Such values are reinforced in the social process. These values then are carried through into a person's way of being. They are put to the test, changed and shaped within the personal, social, cultural and political contexts. The concept of inclusion emerges in the process of social engagement, whether this is in or out of formal schooling, and in relation to the exclusionary pressures faced. The discrepancy between people's expectations and aspirations based on the inclusive values they may hold and the reality of the challenges they face can create a force that drives them to become active agents for social change. This is the struggle that we hear in many of our stories.

Therefore, the conceptualisation of inclusion is dependent on specific social contexts. In the stories there are examples of this in relation to individual professional experiences and professional education. In the case of mothers and children, this is exemplified through their interactions with the professional world.

The personal as well as professional and social contexts have a crucial impact on how this is played out in individual experiences. We appear to struggle within our contexts to understand our own roles and responsibilities towards inclusion, and the roles and responsibilities of others. It therefore becomes imperative that we need to enable a space and time for such an understanding to develop.

Positive contributions to inclusive school communities can be found where individuals are empowered to recognise and express their personal values and experiences within a collective context. The challenge then for the community is to simultaneously hold the individual and the collective. There is a constant interplay and re-conceptualisation between the individual and the

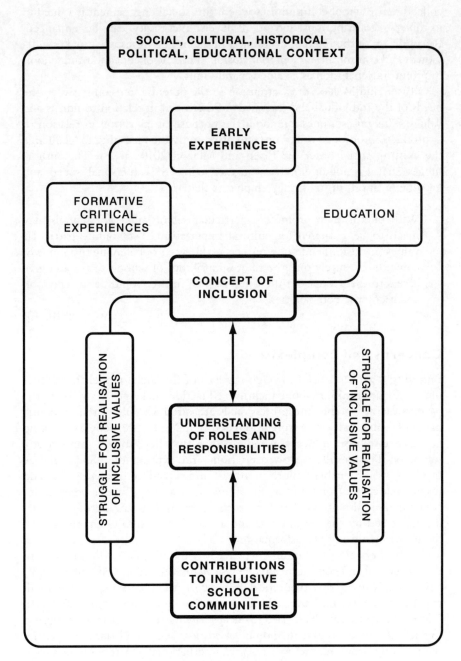

Figure 3.1 Construct map derived from individual contributions.

collective. In school communities where this social engagement is valued in its diverse contributions and at all levels, inclusivity can be enhanced. Recognition of the interconnectedness of diverse beings is what makes individuals and communities open to inclusion. The role of education and schools in promoting inclusion as a value is paramount.

O'Brien and Mcleod draw attention to the potential tension between the needs of the individual and the needs of the social in relation to norms and values. This raises a question about the purpose of education in relation to 'reproduction of social order' or facilitating individual learning to 'challenge the existing social order' (O'Brien and Mcleod 2010: 37–8). The authors suggest that it is not an either/or. Further, with PSHE (personal, social, and health education) in sight, they emphasise that:

> With pluralism to promote a particular set of values for schools may mean to be criticised for cultural imperialism. Yet holding particular values (inclusion) and knowing acceptable ways of behaving in a range of contexts . . . surely must be the responsibility of schools to try and give access to these values to their pupils. The future would be to reflect on and recognise complexities.
>
> (ibid.: 2010: 40)

Concerns and complexities

Engaging with the stories through the lens of the social model that frames much of our thinking about inclusive education makes us realise that the barriers facing parents and professionals are often a result of the predominance of individualistic interpretations of difference. Hence, people's thinking gets trapped within a 'needs' paradigm that can offer limited, minimalistic solutions. This results in low aspirations and expectations. Social model thinking would enable a more thorough understanding of the barriers and inspire search for solutions within the school and the wider community contexts. It is also about enriching each other's understanding of the social barriers faced by the community and a collective commitment to remove these barriers through transformation.

The barriers most commonly perceived by individuals are located within the attitudinal and communicative, physical and organisational domains. We have already used this theoretical framework to understand one school's experiences with inclusive education in Finland (Tarr et al. 2011). In Figures 3.2 and 3.3 we have tried to encapsulate most of the perceived barriers to inclusion as expressed in individual stories. We found stark similarities with findings from our previous research internationally. Although the social, political and cultural contexts of our recent study of a specific school in Finland are quite different, there appears to be a significant overlap in relation to concerns and complexities facing the professionals involved. The ways

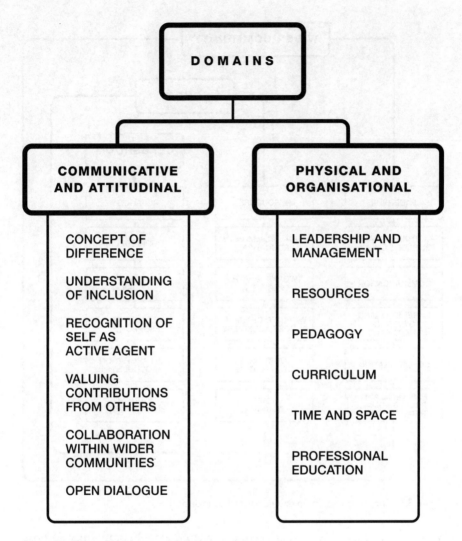

Figure 3.2 Theoretical framework and main themes.

in which barriers are experienced across contexts may differ, but the areas where barriers to inclusion persist show notable similarities.

Collective contribution

In the context of school communities, the questions of voice and credible knowledge are closely linked with the questions of power and agency. The stories reflected concerns about systems, structures, hierarchy and varied levels of engagement for each context. These were different in each case

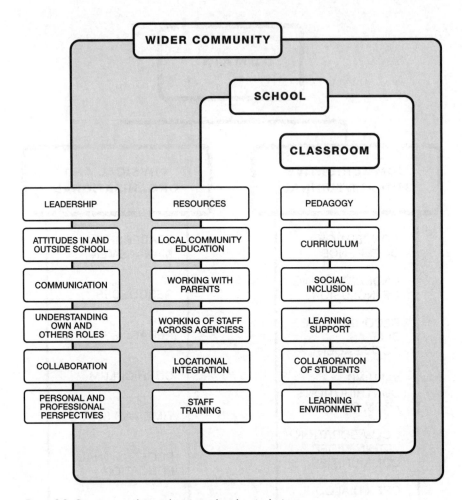

Figure 3.3 Concerns and complexities related to inclusion.

within each storyteller's experience of a specific school community. Whose voice and whose power were questions that caused collective concern. Views and perspectives of members in school communities appeared to be differentially explored and listened to.

> How people are known, described and situated – whose story dominates the script and the consequent social and educational trajectories – is central to the development of inclusive education thinking, writing and practice. Put simply, inclusive education, according to this conception, becomes a field of cultural politics with the objective of social reconstruction.
>
> (Slee 2008: 106)

We were concerned that the child, who is the central purpose of education, is least heard and therefore least powerful, particularly where her/his perspectives are regarded as difficult to obtain.

In terms of power, the status of different professionals allied to various disciplines seems to dictate their role, function and possible contribution to a school community. Our reflections on learning from the stories prompted us to create an abstract visual representation of the possible distribution of power in a school community in a UK context (Figure 3.4). We included only the positions of those who participated in the research for this book and therefore the figure is only specific to this text.

The top and bottom of the hierarchy of power were least disputed. The middle actors, mainly professionals and governors on the periphery, were those who appeared to act as advocates for children and families. The levels of power circulate between such professionals and paraprofessionals depending on their assumed responsibility, knowledge and understanding, personal capacity and specific insights into school environments.

The diverse collection of stories illuminates the potential of school communities to develop through learning from each other and working together in a vibrant learning environment. All participants have the capacity to engage and contribute in the collective learning process. We see such engagement and contribution as fundamental parts of what we may call 'inclusive pedagogy'.

Inclusive pedagogy in this sense could be linked to various proposed theoretical models for learning: the social constructivist approaches to learning (Vygotsky 1983); a 1996 UNESCO document, *Learning: the treasure within*, which focuses on learning to know, to do, to work together and to be; and a model put forward by Rouse (2008) that has been used to theorise about the professional development of student teachers, referring to inclusive pedagogy as a reciprocal triangular relationship between beliefs, knowledge and action. Inclusive pedagogy we construct as personal and professional engagement: an ongoing dialogue as a foundation for knowledge creation. Therefore our emphasis is on 'how' we learn and grow together and on learning from and through collective experiences within the wider community.

So what about the transformative action? What change can be brought about by such insight? For us, this will mean taking forward and promoting this inclusive pedagogy wherever possible. In terms of inclusive school communities, the transformative potential is that 'listening to the various stakeholders and of allowing the voices of people at the sharp end of inclusive practice' to be heard holds opportunity to 'be instrumental in the development of such services' (Jones 2003: 159).

The concerns and complexities outlined in Figure 3.3 above are linked to the questions of hierarchy, power and agency. For example, the nature of the physical space that people are allowed to occupy impacts on the potential contributions that people are able to make to school communities. It is also

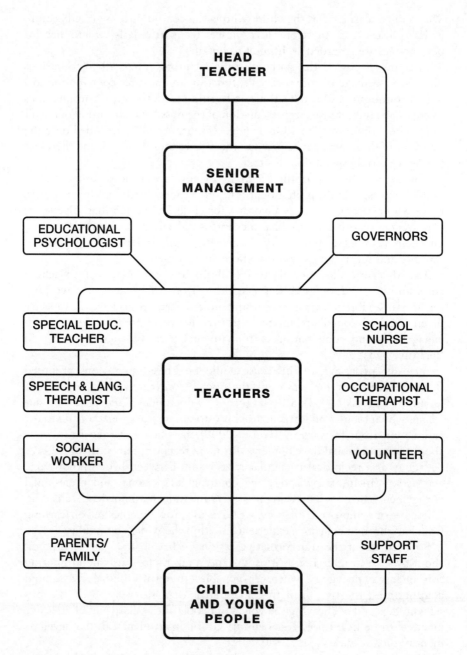

Figure 3.4 School community hierarchy.

about the interpersonal spaces where dialogue and exchange can take place easily and are encouraged. For example, Cole writes 'Yet, if progress is to be made at all in the inclusion of all children, we have to blur the boundaries of home and school and create spaces where we can discuss and differ but develop our ideas' (Cole 2007: 171).

The leadership of a school community holds the potential power to initiate and enable inclusive processes. Their power can have an impact on the development of attitudes and appears to be crucial for the generation, distribution and management of resources. The leadership can be instrumental in creating an ethos for informal and formal professional education, too.

Inclusive school communities

Our experience, reflections and thoughts provoked by this research process enhanced our understanding of what may be some potential markers of inclusive school communities. Inclusive school communities would demonstrate commitment to:

- valuing communication as a fundamental human process of engagement and seeking to communicate with all stakeholders; communication as understood in a multidimensional and multimodal way;
- an aptitude to exploration and creativity requiring flexibility of thinking and being in a wide range of contexts, and the ability to live with uncertainties;
- believing in the power of collaborative democratic processes and practising such principles;
- engaging in/holding confrontation and exchanging different perspectives in a constructive and reflective manner;
- understanding, respecting and trusting in individual and collective potentials recognising different background, experience, knowledge and skills, and enabling everyone to contribute to the best of their personal and professional capacities;
- providing an outward-looking convivial environment which welcomes all professionals and community members to take part in the educational process.

Through the book-writing process, we learnt that we are often driven to search for 'the right way' out of ourselves and do not give enough credit to our own feelings, understanding and experience. Once we learn to respect ourselves sufficiently to be able to reflect on, express and share our experience as our own learning/knowledge, then we can engage with the learning of others in a respectful way. It works reciprocally: through dialogue and respectful engagement with others, one is empowered to give credit and to voice individual experience/perspective as credible knowledge.

In conclusion, we believe that learning is an ongoing process and the more one engages and reflects on the stories in this book, the more one can enhance one's understanding of the diversity of perspectives on inclusion and inclusive school communities. Far from wanting to put a cap on others' learning by proposing transferrable models or frameworks, we have summarised our experience and learning points and hope that readers will be prompted by this text to do the same.

References

Alderson, P. (2008) *Young children's rights: Exploring beliefs, principles and practice.* London: Jessica Kingsley.

Allan, J. (2008) *Rethinking inclusive education.* New York: Springer-Verlag.

Armstrong, D. (2003) *Experiences of special education: Re-evaluating policy and practice through life stories.* Oxford: Routledge.

Armstrong, D. (2005) 'Reinventing "inclusion": New Labour and the cultural politics of special education', *Oxford Review of Education*, 31(1), 135–51.

Armstrong, A.C., Armstrong, D. and Spandagou, I. (2010) *Inclusive education: International policy and practice.* London: SAGE.

Azzopardi, A. (2008) *Career guidance for persons with disability.* Valletta: Euroguidance.

Azzopardi, A. (2011a) Special issue editorial: 'Creating inclusive communities', *International Journal of Inclusive Education*, 15(1), 1–5.

Azzopardi, A. (2011b) 'Conceptualising discursive communities: Developing community in contemporary society', *International Journal of Inclusive Education*, 15(1), 179–93

Baginsky, M. (ed.) (2008) *Safeguarding children and schools.* London: Jessica Kingsley.

Bakhtin, M.M. (1981) *The dialogic imagination: Four essays.* Austin: University of Texas.

Barnes, C. (2002) 'Emancipatory disability research: Project or process?', *Journal of Research on Special Educational Needs*, 1(2).

Barton, L. (2005) 'Special Educational Needs: An alternative look (A Response to Warnock M. 2005: "Special Educational Needs – A new look")', accessed online at: http://www.leeds.ac.uk/disability-studies/archiveuk/barton/Warnock.pdf

Beresford, B., Rabiee, P. and Sloper, P. (2007) 'Priorities and perceptions of disabled children and young people and their parents regarding outcomes from support services', DH 2147, University of York Social Policy Research Unit.

Booth, T. (2003) 'Inclusion in the city: Concepts and contexts', in Potts, P (ed.), *Inclusion in the City.* Oxford: Routledge.

Booth, T and Ainscow, M. (2011) *Index for inclusion. Developing learning and participation in schools.* Bristol: CSIE.

Boyle, C. and Lauchlan, F. (2009) 'Applied psychology and the case for individual casework: Some reflections on the role of the educational psychologist', *Educational Psychology in Practice*, 25(1), 71–84.

Bronfenbrenner, U. (1979) *The ecology of human development: Experiments by nature and design.* Cambridge, MA: Harvard University Press.

Buber, M. (1959) *I and thou*. Edinburgh: Clark.

Casey, C. (1995) *Work, self and society: After industrialism*. Oxford: Routledge.

CLG (Communities and Local Government) (2006) *Commission on Integration and Cohesion – Our shared future*. Wetherby: Communities and Local Government Publications.

Clough, N. and Tarr, J. (2011) Researching intercultural dimensions within innovative pedagogies', *Querer Saber* No 4, 2010, Instituto Paulo Freire de Portugal, University of Porto.

Cole, B.A. (2004) *Mother–teacher's insights into inclusion*. London: David Fulton.

Cole, B.A. (2007) 'Mothers, gender and inclusion in the context of home-school relations', *Support for Learning*, 22(4), 165–73.

Curcic, S., Gabel, V.Z., Zeitlin, V., Cribaro-DiFatta, S. and Glarner, C. (2011) 'Policy and challenges of building schools as inclusive communities', *International Journal of Inclusive Education*, 15(1), 117–18.

CWDC (Children's Workforce Development Council) (2005) 'The common assessment framework'. Leeds: CWDC.

CWDC (Children's Workforce Development Council) (2009) 'Social workers: Their work with children, young people and their families'. http://www.cwdcouncil.org.uk/search?q=social+work+task+force accessed 12.6.2011.

CWDC (Children's Workforce Development Council) (2010) 'The common core of skills and knowledge: At the heart of what you do'. Leeds: CWDC.

DCSF (Department for Children, Schools and Families) (2007) 'The children's plan: Building brighter futures', Cm 7280. London: The Stationery Office.

DCSF (Department for Children, Schools and Families) (2009) 'Deployment and impact of support staff in schools – the impact of support staff in schools'. Research Report DCSF-RR148, Institute of Education, University of London DCSF.

DCSF (Department for Children, Schools and Families)/CLG (Communities and Local Government) (2007) *Guidance on the duty to promote community cohesion*. Nottingham: DfCSF Publications.

Dean, C., Dyson, A., Gallannaugh, F., Howes, A. and Raffo, C. (2007) 'Schools, governors and disadvantage', Research Report. York: Joseph Rowntree Foundation.

DfE (Department for Education) (2011a) 'The Munro review of child protection: Final report – a child-centred system, presented to Parliament by the Secretary of State for Education by Command of Her Majesty'. London: DfE.

DfE (Department for Education) (2011b) 'Support and aspiration: A new approach to special educational needs and disability', Green Paper. London: DfE.

DfEE (Department for Education and Employment) (2000) 'Sure Start: Making a difference for children and families'. London: DfEE.

DfES (Department for Education and Science) (1978) 'Special Educational Needs', report of the Committee of Enquiry into the Education of Handicapped Children and Young People, Cmnd 7212. London: The Stationery Office.

DfES (Department for Education and Skills) (2001) 'Special Educational Needs: Code of practice'. London: DfES.

DfES (Department for Education and Skills) (2002) 'Time for standards: Reforming the school workforce'. Nottingham: DfES.

DfES (Department for Education and Skills) (2004) 'Every child matters: Change for children'. London: DfES.

DfES (Department for Education and Skills) (2007a) 'Diversity and citizenship curriculum review'. London: DfES.

DfES (Department for Education and Skills) (2007b) 'Every parent matters'. London: DfES accessed online at http://www.teachernet.gov.uk/everyparentmatters.

Dobrev, Z. (1979) *Differentiating between children with temporary developmental impairment and those with mental retardation*. Sofia: Sofia University Press.

Dobrev, Z. (1984) 'About the education of children with anomalies', *Narodna Prosveta* 7.

Dobrev, Z. (1992) *Foundations of Defectology*. Sofia: Sofia University Press.

DoH (Department of Health) (2002) 'Requirements for social work training'. London: DoH.

DoH (Department of Health) (2004) 'National service framework for children, young people and maternity services: The mental health and psychological wellbeing of children and young people'. London: DoH.

DoH (Department of Health) (2007) 'National service framework for children, young people and maternity services: Core standards'. London: DoH.

DoH (Department of Health) (2010) 'Equity and excellence: Liberating the NHS', White Paper. London: DoH.

Dukes, C. (2007) *Working with parents of children with special educational needs*. London: Paul Chapman.

Elkins, J., van Kraayenoord, C.E. and Jobling, A. (2003) 'Parents' attitudes to inclusion of their children with special needs', *Journal of Research in Special Educational Needs*, 3(2), 122–9.

Farrell, P., Woods, K., Lewis, S., Squires, G., Rooney, S. and O'Connor, M. (2006) 'A review of the functions and contribution of educational psychologists in England and Wales in light of "Every child matters: Change for children".' Nottingham: DfES.

Florian, L. (2008) 'Special or inclusive education: Future trends', *British Journal of Special Education*, 35(4), 202–8.

Flutter, J. and Ruddock, J. (2004) *Consulting pupils: What's in it for schools?* Oxford: Routledge.

Frederickson, N. and Cline, T. (2009) *Special educational needs, inclusion and diversity*. Maidenhead: Open University Press.

Freire, P. (1971) *Pedagogy of the oppressed*. New York: Continuum.

Giangreco, M.F. (2010) 'Utilization of teacher assistants in inclusive schools: Is it the kind of help that helping is all about?', *European Journal of Special Needs Education*, 25(4), 341–5.

Green, A., Preston, J. and Janmaat, G. (2006) *Education, equality and social cohesion*. London: Palgrave.

Griffiths, M. (2003) *Action for social justice in education: Fairly different*. Maidenhead: Open University Press.

Grossman, D.L. (2008) 'Democracy, citizenship education and inclusion: A multi-dimensional approach', *Prospects*, 38, 35–46.

Gunter, H. and Thomson, P. (2007) 'Learning about student voice', *Support for Learning*, 22(4), 181–8.

Hargreaves, A. (1993) *Changing teachers, changing times: Teachers' work and culture in the post modern age*. New York: Continuum.

Hart, R. (1992) *Children's participation: From tokenism to citizenship*. Florence: UNICEF.

Heshusius, L. (2004) 'Reading Heshusius', in Gallagher, D., Heshuius, L., Iano, R.P. and Skrtic, T.M., *Challenging orthodoxy in special education: Dissenting voices*, pp 27–61. Denver: Love Publishing.

Howes, A. (2003) 'The impact of paid adult support on the participation and learning of pupils in mainstream schools', EPPI-Centre, Social Science Research Unit, Institute of Education, University of London.

Jones, P. (2003) 'The synergy between research and practice: Listening to the perspectives of key stakeholders about the development of an inclusive early years service', *Journal of Research in Special Educational Needs*, 3(2), 159–175.

Laluvein, J. (2010) 'Variations on a theme: Parents and teachers talking', *Support for Learning*, 25(4), 194–200.

Lamb, B. (2009) *Lamb Inquiry: Special educational needs and parental confidence.* Nottingham: DCSF Publications.

MacConville, R. (2007) *Looking at inclusion: Listening to the voices of young people.* London: Paul Chapman.

Mittler, P. (2008) 'Planning for the 2040s: Everybody's business', *British Journal of Special Education*, 35(1), 3–10.

Mukherjee, S., Lightfoot, J. and Sloper, P. (2001) 'Communicating about pupils in mainstream school with special health needs: The NHS perspective', *Child: Care, Health and Development*, 28(1), 21–7.

Munro, E. (2011) 'The Munro review of child protection interim report: The child's journey', http://www.education.gov.uk/munroreview/downloads/ Munrointerimreport.pdf (accessed 18.6.2011).

O'Brien, J. and Mcleod, G. (2010) *The social agenda of the school.* Edinburgh: Dunedin Academic Press.

Oliver, M. (1990) *The politics of disablement.* London: Macmillan.

Oliver, M. (1994) *Politics and language: Understanding the disability discourse.* Sheffield: University of Sheffield.

Oliver, M. (1996) *Understanding disability: From theory to practice.* Basingstoke: Macmillan.

Oliver, M. (2002) 'Emancipatory Research: A vehicle for social transformation or policy development', Annual Disability Research Seminar hosted by The National Disability Authority and The Centre for Disability Studies, University College Dublin.

Oliver, M. and Barnes, C. (1998) *Disabled People and Social Policy – From Exclusion to Inclusion.* London: Longman.

Pinkus, S. (2003) 'All talk and no action: Transforming the rhetoric of parent–professional partnership into practice', *Journal of Research in Special Educational Needs*, 3(2), 128–40.

PPEL (Parents as Partners in Early Learning project) (2007) 'Parental involvement: A snapshot of policy and practice'. PPEL project phase 1 report Sure Start Programme. *http://nso.archive.teachfind.com/node/84956.*

PricewaterhouseCoopers (2001) 'Teacher workload study'. London: DfES.

Raphael Reed, L. (2010) Seminar presentation: 'Developing a dialogic and respectful learning community', to Education Department at University of the West of England Bristol.

Rouse, M. (2008) 'Developing inclusive practice: A role for teachers and teacher education?', *Education in the North*, 16, 6–11.

Schneider, J. (2007) *Supporting children and families: Lessons from Sure Start for evidence-based practice in health, social care and education.* London: Jessica Kingsley.

Scottish Executive (2002) 'Review of Provision of Educational Psychology Services in Scotland (Currie Report)'. Glasgow: SCQF.

Sidorkin, A. (1999) *Beyond discourse: Education, the self and dialogue.* New York: SUNY Press.

Slee, R. (2008) 'Beyond special and regular schooling? An inclusive education reform agenda', *International Studies in Sociology of Education*, 18(2), 99–116.

Slee, R. (2011) *Irregular school: Exclusion, schooling and inclusive education.* Oxford: Routledge.

Stanley, L. and Wise, S. (1993) *Breaking out again: Feminist ontology and epistemology,* Oxford: Routledge.

Stenhouse, L. (1978) 'Case study and case records: Towards a contemporary history of education', *British Educational Research Journal*, 4(2).

SWTF (Social Work Task Force) (2009) 'Building a safe, confident future – final report'. London: DCSF.

Tarr, J. (1997) 'Dramatic liaisons: Collaboration between special and mainstream schools', in Dwyfor Davies, J. and Garner, P. (eds), *At the crossroads: special educational needs and teacher education.* London: David Fulton.

Tarr, J. (2009) 'Integrating professional roles in early years around children's lives and learning', in Eke, R., Butcher, H. and Lee, M. (eds), *Whose childhood is it?* London: Continuum.

Tarr, J. and Thomas, G. (2000) 'Inclusive education and the arts', in Kear, M. and Callaway, G. (eds), *Improving teaching and learning in the Arts.* London: Falmer.

Tarr, J., Tsokova, D. and Takkunen, U.M. 'Insights into inclusive education through a small Finnish case study of an inclusive school context', *International Journal of Inclusive Education.* DOI: 10.1080/13603116.2010.502947, online at http://www.tandfonline.com/do:/abs/10.1080/13603116.2010.502947

TDA (Teacher Development Agency) (2003) 'Professional standards for HLTA status'. http://www.tda.gov.uk/school-leader/developing-staff/hlta/professional-standards.aspx.

TDA (Teacher Development Agency) (2008) 'Qualified teacher status standards' http://www.tda.gov.uk/training-provider/itt/qts-standards-itt-requirements/guidance/qts-standards.aspx accessed 5.5.2011.

TDA (Teacher Development Agency) (2011) 'Teachers Standards effective from 1st September 2012'. http://media.education.gov.uk/assets/files/pdf/t/teachers%20standards.pdf accessed 8.8.2011.

Thomas, G. (1998) 'The myth of rational research', *British Educational Research Journal*, 24(2), 141–61.

Thomas, G. and Loxley, A. (2001) *Deconstructing special education and constructing inclusion.* Buckingham: Open University Press.

Thomas, G., Walker, B. and Webb, J. (1998) *The making of the inclusive school.* Oxford: Routledge.

Tomlinson, J. (1996) 'Inclusive learning', the report of the Learning Difficulties and/or Disabilities Committee of the Further Education Funding Council London: TSO.

Touraine, A. (2000) *Can we live together? Equality and difference*, Cambridge: Polity Press.

TSO (1995) 'Disability Discrimination Act'. London: The Stationery Office.

TSO (2001) 'Special Educational Needs and Disability Act'. London: The Stationery Office

TSO (2004) 'Children Act'. London: The Stationery Office.

TSO (2005) 'Disability Discrimination Act'. London: The Stationery Office.

TSO (2010) 'Equality Act'. London: The Stationery Office.

Tsokova, D. (2002) 'Learning support: What does it have to contribute to inclusion?' International Seminar – FNPP, Kiten, Bulgaria.

Tsokova, D. (2007a) 'Inclusion of children with SLD: What can we learn from others' perspectives?' *Bulgarian Journal of Special Education*, 1/2007.

Tsokova, D. (2007b) 'Values and inclusion of children with special educational needs', international conference FNPP – Sofia University and Ministry of Education and Science of Bulgaria.

Tsokova, D. (2008) 'Collaborative work for inclusive education', in Dobrev, Z. and Evgenieva, E. (eds), *Inclusive education and resource teachers*. Sofia: Sofia University Press.

Tsokova, D. (2009) 'Integration and inclusion of children with learning difficulties: What direction are we taking?', in Dobrev, Z. (ed.), *Contemporary trends in the integration and education of children with learning disabilities*. Sofia: Sofia University Press.

Tsokova, D. (2010) 'About the future of special and inclusive education', *Bulgarian Journal of Special Education*, 12/2010, 5–12.

Tzokova, D. and Garner, P. (1996) 'Special educational needs: A teacher education initiative in Bulgaria', *Journal of Practice in Education for Development*, 2(2), 75–80.

UNESCO (1994) 'The Salamanca statement and framework for action on special needs education'. Paris: UNESCO.

UNESCO (1996) 'Learning: the treasure within', Report to UNESCO of the International Commission on Education for the Twenty-First Century. Paris: UNESCO.

United Nations (1989) 'Convention on the rights of the child'. New York: United Nations.

United Nations (2006) 'Convention on the rights of persons with disabilities'. New York: United Nations.

Vincett, K., Cremin, H. and Thomas, G. (2005) *Teachers and assistants working together*. Maidenhead: Open University Press.

Vygotsky, L.S. (1983) *Collected works: Vol. 5. Foundations of defectology*. Moscow: Izdatel'stvo Pedagogika (in Russian).

Warnock, M. (2005) 'Special educational needs: A new look'. London: Philosophy of Education Society of Great Britain.

Webster, R., Blatchford, P., Bassett, P., Brown, P., Martin, C. and Russell, A. (2010a) 'Double standards and first principles: Framing teaching assistant support for pupils with special educational needs', *European Journal of Special Needs Education*, 25(4), 319–36.

Webster, R., Blatchford, P., Bassett, P., Brown, P., Martin, C. and Russell, A. (2010b) 'Engaging with the question "should teaching assistants have a pedagogical role?"', *European Journal of Special Needs Education*, 25(4), 347–8.

Wolfendale, S. (1997) *Working with parents of SEN children after the Code of Practice.* London: David Fulton.

Wolfendale, S. (2002) *Parent partnership services for special educational needs: Celebrations and challenges.* London: David Fulton.

Young, I.M. (2000) *Justice and the politics of difference.* New York: Princeton University Press.

Index

Page numbers in **bold** refer to figures

Action on Reflective Practice 95
Allan, J. 12
Apert Syndrome: mother's perspective
    30–3; young people's perspective
    33–4
applied behavioural analysis (ABA)
    programme 25, 27–8
Armstrong, D. 11
Arts Integration Project 101
autism: mother's perspective 21–3,
    25–8; young people's perspective
    23–5, 28–9
Azzoparrdi, A. 2, 5–6

Baginsky, M. 18
Barnardos 16, 61–5
Barton, L. 5, 12
Beresford, B. 11
Blunkett, D. 10
Booth, T. 1
Bourdieu, P. 38
Bulgarian Journal of Special Education
    96

Casey, C. 7
Children Act (2004) 20
Cole, B. A. 12, 115
Commission on Integration and
    Cohesion 9
Common Assessment Framework 20
Common Core of Skills and
    Knowledge 20
Curcic, S. 2

defectology 93–4
Disability and Society 5

Disability Discrimination Act (1995) 10
Dobrev, Z. 93, 94

Education Act (1981) 10
educational psychologist 66–72; early
    years 66–7, 70–2; role 16–17; training
    tutor 67–70
emotional and behavioural difficulties
    (EBD) 43
Equality Act (2010) 10
Every Child Matters 9, 11, 17, 19, 39
Every Child Matters: Change for Children
    103
Every Parent Matters 11

Freire, P. 45

governor: primary school 58–61; role
    16; secondary school 55–8
Griffiths, M. 8
Grossman, D. L. 5
Gunter, H. 11, 14

Hargreaves, A. 57
Hart, R. 57
health practitioner 81–91; occupational
    therapist 84–7; role 18–19; school
    nurse 87–91; speech and language
    therapist 81–4
Heshusius, L. 108

inclusion 5–6, 9; concerns and
    complexities **112**
inclusive education 1, 10–11; children
    with Down syndrome 36; context
    9–19; context for inclusive school

communities 19–20; methodology 6; reflections on learning from joint experiences 104–5; research ethics 8–9; research process 7–8; research through perspectives 3–5; stories and reflections 92–104; theoretical framework 5–6; UNESCO Salamanca Statement 10
inclusive pedagogy 113
inclusive school communities 1, 10, 115–16; context for 19–20; research through perspectives 3–5
International Journal of Inclusive Education 2

Laluvein, J. 13
Lamb Inquiry (2009) 12
Learning: the treasure within 113
learning points 107–16; collective contribution 111–15; concerns and complexities 110–11; construct map **109**; inclusive school communities 115–16; individual contributions 107–10; school community hierarchy **114**; theoretical framework ad main themes **111**
learning support assistant (LSA) 15–16, 36; primary school 48–50, 53–4
Loxley, A. 14

MacConville, R. 11
Mcleod G. 110
Mittler, P. 12
Munro, E. 18

narrative 6
National Service Framework 18

O'Brien, J. 110
occupational therapist 84–7
Oliver, M. 5

parent: role 11–13
professional dependency 39

Raphael Reed, L. 3–4
research ethics 8–9

research process 7–8
Rouse, M. 113

school nurse 87–91
Sidorkin, A. 4
Slee, R. 4, 6, 112
social cohesion 9
social constructivist approach 5
social worker 73–80; disabled children's team 76–8; Early Intervention Social Care Worker 73–6; qualification 18; residential special school 78–80; role 17–18
Special Educational Needs Code of Practice 10
speech and language therapist 81–4
Stanley, L. 8
Stenhouse, L. 6
support staff: LSA in a primary school 48–50, 53–4; role 14–16; TA in a special school 50–3

teacher: inner city secondary school 37–43; primary school 35–7; role 13–14; special school 43–7
teaching assistant 14–16; special school 50–3
The Pedagogy of the Oppressed 45
Thomas, G. 1, 14
Thomson, P. 11, 14
Touraine, A. 4

UNESCO Salamanca Statement 9, 10
United Nations Convention on Children's Rights (UNCRC) 9
United Nations Convention on Rights of Persons with Disability 9

Vincett, K. 15
voluntary and community sector: role 16
Vygotsky, L. S. 93–4

Warnock Report 10
Webster, R. 15
Wise, S. 8

Young, I. M. 6